eva's kitchen

eva's kitchen

cooking with love for family & friends

eva longoria

WITH MARAH STETS

CLARKSON POTTER/PUBLISHERS

NEW YORK

Copyright © 2011 by Eva Longoria Parker
Food photography © 2011 by Ben Fink
Portrait photography © 2011 by Randall Slavin
Photographs on page 24 copyright © 2011 by Maile Wilson

Published in the United States by Clarkson Potter/Publishers,
an imprint of the Crown Publishing Group, a division of
Random House, Inc., New York.
www.crownpublishing.com
www.clarksonpotter.com

CLARKSON POTTER is a trademark and
POTTER with colophon is a registered
trademark of Random House, Inc.

Library of Congress
Longoria, Eva.
Eva's kitchen : cooking with love for family and
friends / Eva Longoria.—1st ed.
Includes index.
1. Cooking.   2. Entertaining.   3. Cookbooks.
I. Title.
TX714.P3745   2011
641.5—dc22   2010035479

ISBN 978-0-307-71933-1

Printed in the United States of America

Design by Jennifer K. Beal Davis

10 9 8 7 6 5 4 3

First Edition

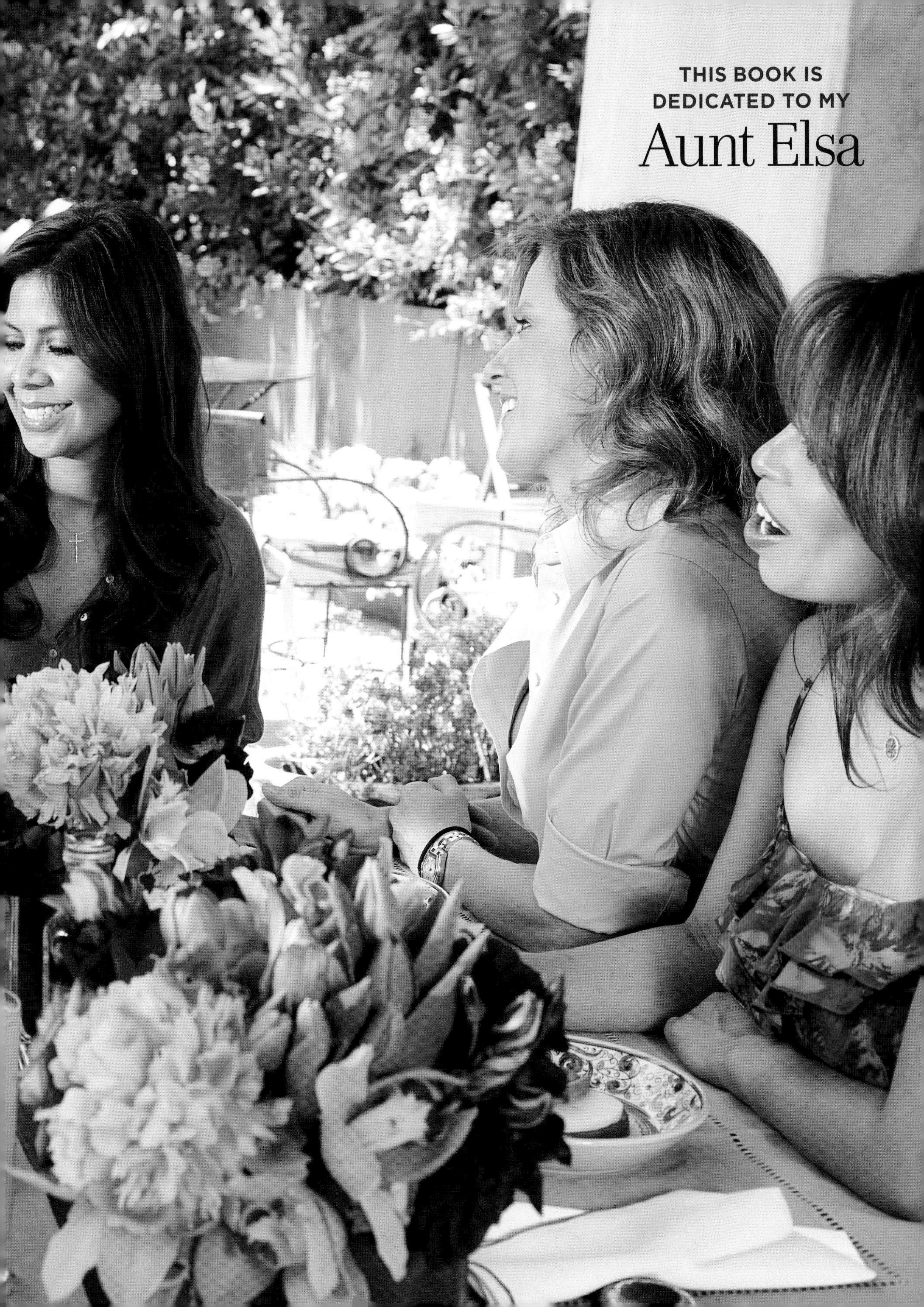

THIS BOOK IS
DEDICATED TO MY

Aunt Elsa

contents

Introduction 8

Appetizers   15

Soups & Salads   41

Fish Main Courses   67

Poultry Main Courses   77

Beef Main Courses   99

Delectable Sides   121

Dressings & Sauces   157

Tortillas, Biscuits & Quick Breads   169

Desserts   183

Drinks   213

Resources 220

Acknowledgments 221

Index 222

introduction

My love affair with cooking started long ago, but I remember it so clearly. When I was about six years old, my mom was leaving for work early one morning and I told her I was hungry. "So cook something!" she answered. I vividly remember pulling up a chair to the stove and turning it on with a match. (I know—dangerous, but it was a different time!) I selected the smallest frying pan I could find because I wanted to cook one egg. Not eggs, just one egg. I cracked the egg on the edge of the pan, as I'd seen my mom do effortlessly many times before, and emptied it into the frying pan.

Of course, the pan was full of eggshell. I didn't use any butter or oil, so the egg stuck everywhere. I can't even remember now what it tasted like, but I can recall the feeling of accomplishment I had after cooking that egg. I found it empowering and energizing. I was hooked from that day forward.

I wanted to learn everything! I wanted my little EASY-BAKE Oven to make casseroles like my mom's. I wanted my lemonade stand to have more flavor options than just lemon. And for Christmas I wanted my own hand mixer! I eventually graduated from cooking an egg to making my own spaghetti sauce.

I have my family to thank for my cooking skills and the inspiration they gave me to begin my own culinary journey. My dad was a big believer in never eating fast food, so we were not allowed to have it. And nothing ever went to waste. I grew up on a ranch outside of Corpus Christi, Texas, and throughout my childhood my family grew our own vegetables and raised our own chickens. Every day my mom cooked with garden-fresh *calabasa* (squash), carrots, and beans, and freshly laid eggs. Every last bit of that garden's harvest was always used, and any trimmings went right to the compost pile. She worked full-time as a special education teacher; took care of my oldest sister, who is developmentally disabled; and had three other daughters to drive all over town to cheerleading, band practice, work, and everywhere else busy teenage girls need to go. But in spite of it all, she always managed to have dinner on the table every night at 6 P.M. for my dad. This was such an important lesson in my life. The fact that my mother clearly reveled in taking care of her family in addition to having a career inspired me to be the same way. I cannot count the number of times that I've found myself in a Gucci dress and heels—with full hair and makeup, about to run out to an event—pulling a roasted chicken out of the oven in order to make sure that my family is fed before leaving the house to face a hundred photographers on a red carpet.

I remember cooking a Cuban dish all day (because it takes eight hours) and then running off to a red carpet event where an interviewer actually said to me, "You smell good, like food!"

"Oh, that's *comino*," I answered, using the Spanish word for cumin. "I was cooking Ropa Vieja all day."

It made me laugh, but at the same time it reminded me that my family comes first, and my acting second.

And then there was my Aunt Elsa, who was the biggest influence on my cooking. She passed away a few years ago and I miss her still. She was a professional caterer and her kitchen was always bustling with activity for a party or event she had coming up. She was so inspiring, and a deep well of information. A vault of recipes lay at the tip of her tongue. And she, like my parents, knew how to make ingredients *last*. Put a chicken in Elsa's hands on Monday, and you'd eat a bit of it every day for a week; she used the meat, the bones, the wing tips, everything! Because Elsa was a caterer, she had mastered the art of cooking for large groups, as well as cooking the bases of various dishes and freezing them for later use. For example, she made the most delicious biscuits by adding water to a two-gallon bag of base that she kept in the freezer (I share her recipe on page 177). She did this with bases for chili, tomato sauce, cookie dough, punch, and tamales. She never measured, a sin I am guilty of as well. In fact, as a dedicated "handful of this, pinch of that" kind of cook, the hardest part of writing this cookbook was learning how to measure!

I believe it is because of Elsa that I love when food is beautifully presented. Since most of what she prepared had to look as good as it tasted, Aunt Elsa had an eye for what food needed to make it visually pop. She could employ simple touches like trimming the crusts off tea sandwiches and more elaborate flourishes like serving fruit salad in a watermelon that she hollowed out so that the bright pink interior shone against the vivid white and green rind. I have her to thank (or to blame) for my obsession with collecting lovely servingware, from

tablecloths and napkins to bowls of all sizes, including the adorable jalapeño-shaped bowl I bought in Mexico and in which I always serve pico de gallo so people know it's spicy!

Aunt Elsa was the source of an endless stream of insights, recipes, and beliefs about cooking I've never heard anywhere else. Every day she had a cooking tip for me and she always volunteered it unasked. That's one thing I loved about her: She would teach you things whether or not you wanted to learn them. She would say, "Evita, never put tomatoes in the fridge," or "Always put apples in the fridge," or "Evita, only flip a tortilla once on the *comal*." She

was also a priceless source of practical information like "Use a dampened paper towel to pick up slivers of broken glass." I absorbed everything my Aunt Elsa told me like a sponge, and I share her knowledge with you on these pages. Look throughout the book for her tips, labeled "From Aunt Elsa's Kitchen."

In this book, I am thrilled to share my passion for cooking along with decades' worth of family recipes and culinary tips. I've delved into the boxes of family and personal recipes I've long treasured and offer our family's tried-and-true recipes and techniques for making the world's best homemade tortillas, Mexican rice, guacamole, and Pan de Polvo, to mention but a few.

Those are the foods that are at the base of my own culinary journey, and it was only after I left home that I discovered a vast culinary world beyond the rich food history of Texas and Mexico. I also include here recipes I've devised and modified over the years that build on my heritage but are further inspired by French, Latin American, Italian, and a range of international styles as well as my political and environmental sensibilities. My cooking style has long been influenced by the full range of fabulous cuisines I've sampled and the incredible chefs I've had the privilege of knowing over the years.

Once I was launched on this culinary journey I began to play with ingredients in new ways and more consciously practice the abiding principles I was taught on my family's ranch and in our kitchen—to treat all living beings with dignity and respect and waste nothing the earth has given you. For a year I became a vegetarian, both for my health and to contribute a little less to the stress that meat and poultry production put on the land and people around it. Though I have now returned to eating an omnivorous diet, I definitely learned some important lessons—and great vegetable and bean recipes—during my meat-free days (check out the Delectable Sides chapter, page 121, to see many of the results). I eat much less meat than I once did and I'm careful about what types of meat, poultry, and fish I buy.

As for produce, this awareness extends to the people who grow and harvest our food. I do a lot of advocacy work for the rights of farm workers because I care deeply about how we treat the people who feed us, the citizens of the best-fed nation in the world. The United States is the most prolific agricultural producer on the planet, and it is on the backs of these workers that we maintain that status. There is a simple way that you can help: Buy organic produce. Switching over to even a minimal amount of organic produce means that you are supporting producers whose workers do not handle and inhale the powerful pesticides that conventional farms use regularly. Farm workers should not be exposed to these poisons, and the fact of the matter is you shouldn't ingest this stuff, either. The nonprofit Environmental Working Group produces a list of the conventionally grown fruits and vegetables that have the most pesticides. They've dubbed the worst of these "the dirty dozen." Even if you choose to buy organic versions of just a few of these, you'll be making a difference. We can send the people who produce our food effective messages by where and how we spend our money, so I carefully choose which producers or production methods to support. It's not hard—just check out Resources (page 220) for information on EWG and other great organizations. The more we customers demand conscientiously grown food, the more available and the cheaper it will become.

Ultimately, there are few places I'd rather be than my kitchen. I'm rarely alone there; my kitchen has long been the go-to place for friends and family alike. It is a place to which I benevolently—or, if you ask my family, at times maniacally—single-handedly run. (Unless, of course, we're making *enchiladas*, which go much faster with many hands—most often my sisters', aunts', and mom's.)

Every friend or family member who stops by makes a personal request for one or another of my dishes. In fact, my two restaurants, Beso in Hollywood and Las Vegas, are a direct result of this phenomenon: cooking with love for family and friends. I've always been passionate about cooking for those I care about. But my kitchen is only so big, so it was a natural next step to open a restaurant. (My first idea was to start a first-rate taco stand, a proper *taqueria*, but when I met Chef Todd English and our visions and sensibilities blended, Beso was born.) And now I have written this book to share with you the joy I feel and the delicious food I love to make when I'm in the kitchen. Just as Aunt Elsa always did for me, I'll begin with a few tips and guidelines.

my pantry

SALT

I use coarse, kosher salt for all my savory cooking. Its big grains stick well to the food without soaking in, so you can use less of it and still get a good, salty taste. I use finer table salt for all my baking, when you want the salt to blend right in.

LEMONS AND LIMES

I grew up surrounded by citrus trees, and I love to use lots of lemons and limes in my cooking. I prefer the small lemons I can get when I'm at my Texas and California homes, so you'll see throughout that I call for small lemons, which each yield about 2 tablespoons of juice. If your lemons are larger and produce more juice, simply use fewer of them. I give both the number of lemons and the amount of juice I intend you to use in each case. Similarly, the limes I use give 2 tablespoons of juice; again, use more or fewer limes if yours yield a different amount.

SHORTENING AND BUTTER

Many of the dishes I grew up eating and preparing were made with lard or shortening, two fats that are not as popular as they once were. Although lard gives incomparable flavor and flaky texture to pie crusts, I simply don't use it anymore. I've adapted some recipes, such as Aunt Elsa's Pineapple Upside-Down Cake to include butter, which tastes better. On the other hand, I still use shortening in some recipes, such as Corn Bread (page 181), where the shortening provides lighter texture than butter would and allows the pure flavor of delicious corn meal to come through. I do avoid trans fats, however, so I don't buy the partially hydrogenated shortening that we used when I was a kid. Instead I buy nonhydrogenated palm oil, available at natural food stores, which does not contain trans fats.

VINEGAR, SPICE, AND MAKING EVERYTHING NICE

I love tangy, spicy foods, so you'll see generous use of vinegar, citrus, and spice. I am also a compulsive taste-as-you-go cook. For this book I've created recipes that will work in any kitchen and appeal to a broad range of palates. But I encourage you to taste as *you* go and decide for yourself if what you're making is to your taste.

Growing up having every family meal based on what was growing in our fields, my cooking to this day relies on fresh, seasonal ingredients. But like so many of us, I am very busy, so I have a well-stocked pantry and a good supply of recipes that can be made without a special trip to the grocery store. All of my recipes rest on a foundation of flavorful but easy-to-find ingredients. So please, turn the page and let me join you in your kitchen. Let's start cooking!

appetizers

I like to say that my house is not mine alone. When I am home, I happily share it with all my friends and family who come over almost every day. I wouldn't have it any other way. With so much activity in the house, especially in the kitchen, often I just need something fast and delicious to keep everyone out of my hair while I cook the main course! I love recipes that rely entirely on items that are always in my pantry. When unexpected guests drop by or dinner is taking a little longer to prepare than I had planned, I can whip up a delicious hors d'oeuvre in less than five minutes. For instance, my pantry never runs out of canned beans for Cannellini Beans with Crushed Red Pepper (page 23) or tortilla chips so folks always have something to scoop up tangy Pico de Gallo (page 20) or Chunky Guacamole with Serrano Peppers (page 19) while I turn my focus to the main event. Other times we forgo the main course altogether and prepare a few heartier appetizers instead. I love the communality of this sort of tapas-style eating, where everyone gets a little taste of each delicious thing.

hot artichoke dip

chunky guacamole with serrano peppers

pico de gallo

cannellini beans with crushed red pepper

ants on a log

normandy shrimp

dad's shrimp cocktail

avocado stuffed with shrimp

ceviche

goat cheese balls

tostones

sweet-potato empanadas

argentinean empanadas

hot artichoke dip

I love this dip for company because you can whip it together and put it in the oven just as your guests arrive. In the time it takes to stow their coats and serve them drinks, the dip becomes hot and bubbly and can be brought from the oven straight to serving, trailing along with it an enticing aroma of warm Parmesan cheese and artichokes. If you have time, prepare the dip by processing it in the food processor, place it in the baking dish, cover, and refrigerate it overnight. With time, the flavors blend and become even better. If you don't have that kind of time, don't worry! This is still a creamy, tangy, wonderful dip even when pulled together at the last possible minute.

MAKES ABOUT 2 CUPS

- 1 14-ounce can artichoke hearts, drained and chopped
- 1 cup mayonnaise
- 1 cup grated Parmesan cheese
- ½ teaspoon garlic powder

  Toast Triangles (recipe follows) or assorted crackers, for serving

1. Preheat the oven to 350°F.

2. In a medium mixing bowl, place the artichoke hearts, mayonnaise, Parmesan cheese, and garlic powder. Stir until well blended. Transfer to the work bowl of a food processor and pulse until you get the desired texture.

3. Lightly spray a small baking dish with cooking spray and transfer the mixture into the dish. Bake until hot and bubbly, about 20 minutes. Serve hot with toast triangles or assorted crackers.

toast triangles

These are easy to make. The paprika adds a nice dash of bright color.

- 4 tablespoons (½ stick) unsalted butter, softened, or as needed
- 12 slices day-old white sandwich bread

  Garlic or onion powder

  Sweet paprika

  Kosher salt (optional)

1. Preheat the oven to 300°F.

2. Lightly spread the butter on one side of each slice of bread. Lightly sprinkle with garlic or onion powder, paprika, and salt, if using. Cut each slice into 4 triangles and place on a cookie sheet. Bake until lightly brown and crisp, 15 to 20 minutes. Cool and serve. To store, place the triangles in a storage bag or tin can and keep at room temperature for 2 to 3 days. Recrisp in the oven if necessary after storing.

chunky guacamole with serrano peppers

Among all the dishes I make, this one is definitely a favorite. This is why the batch is so big—no one can stop eating it! I have a few tricks that give my guacamole great flavor and texture. First and most important, I use lemon, not lime, juice. Lemon has a little sweetness that brings out all the other flavors. Also key is that I never skimp on the lemon or the kosher salt. I sometimes laugh that I basically make a salty lemonade for the avocado and other ingredients to swim in—trust me, it makes all the difference! Serrano peppers give it a great kick, much better than jalapeños. And finally, never stir as you add each ingredient to the bowl or the guacamole will become too watery. This is especially beautiful served in a dish that shows off the guacamole's green, white, and red, such as a *molcajete*—a Mexican mortar and pestle—or a bright and fun serving bowl. Serve with tortilla chips for an appetizer or on top of steak, such as in Chili-Rubbed Skirt Steak Tacos (page 102).

MAKES ABOUT 8 CUPS

- 6 ripe avocados, cut into ½-inch dice
- 4 medium ripe tomatoes, cut into ½-inch dice
- 1 large white onion, finely chopped
- ½ bunch of fresh cilantro, leaves chopped
- 1 serrano pepper, finely minced
- Juice from 4 small lemons (about 8 tablespoons)
- 2 teaspoons kosher salt or to taste

1. In a large bowl, place the avocados, tomatoes, onion, cilantro, serrano, lemon juice, and salt. Stir gently until well combined.

2. Transfer to a serving bowl and serve.

FROM AUNT ELSA'S KITCHEN
To keep the guacamole from turning brown, press a pit from one of the avocados into the center of the dish. Remove it before serving.

pico de gallo

I frequently have friends over to play games at my house, and it's become a game night tradition that I put out heaping bowls of Pico de Gallo and guacamole along with a big basket of tortilla chips. Pico de Gallo improves with time and I serve it with chips, of course, but also spooned over any red meat, in tacos, or with scrambled eggs for huevos rancheros.

For an extra chunky salsa, simply mix all the ingredients together without pureeing. Whatever texture you prefer, the burst of fresh flavor this salsa offers depends on using ripe, in-season tomatoes and lime—never lemon—juice. For a spicier salsa, leave some or all of the seeds in the serrano peppers.

MAKES ABOUT 3 CUPS

- 2 medium tomatoes, chopped
- 1 white onion, chopped
- ½ bunch of fresh cilantro, leaves chopped
- 2 serrano peppers, stemmed, seeded, and minced
- Juice of 1 lime (about 2 tablespoons) or to taste
- Kosher salt to taste
- Tortilla chips, for serving

1. In the work bowl of a food processor or blender, place the tomatoes, onion, cilantro, serrano, and lime juice. Pulse until you like the consistency of the salsa. Taste and add additional lime juice, if desired, and salt.

2. Transfer to a small serving bowl and serve with tortilla chips. Pico de gallo can be stored in a tightly covered container in the refrigerator for up to 1 week.

FRESH PEPPERS

There are countless varieties of peppers (also called chiles) available, and aficionados can identify the distinctions of each and every one. For the purpose of this book, I'll highlight just a few that are readily available and always delicious. Bell, serrano, and jalapeño are the three fresh peppers I use most often. (For information on dried chiles, see page 96).

Bell peppers come in a rainbow of colors, from green to red, yellow, orange, and purple. They are crunchy and sweet, with no spicy bite whatsoever. They are welcome additions to dishes like Hungarian Paprika Chicken (page 84) and they are large enough to hold generous amounts of flavorful stuffing, as in Stuffed Green Peppers (page 116).

Serrano peppers have straightforward chile flavor and good heat that is not at all overpowering. About 2 inches long, they are most often green, although you can sometimes find red ones. Serranos are enormously popular in Mexican cooking and absolutely critical in my Chunky Guacamole with Serrano Peppers (page 19) and Pico de Gallo (above).

Finally, green jalapeños are widely available. They can be very hot and have a distinct flavor with grassy, green bell pepper qualities. They zip up VeraCruz Corn (page 151) and Corn Bread (page 181) with bright color, flavor, and heat.

cannellini beans with crushed red pepper

I first had this dish at a restaurant in Florence, Italy. I took a bite and immediately asked the waiter to tell me exactly what was in it. When he told me, I had the same reaction I've had so many times after tasting something delicious in Europe: "That's it?!" I don't know if it comes from wisdom or restraint or both, but Europeans can take the simplest ingredients and extract from them the most exquisite flavors. My introduction to this dish coincided with my one-year stint as a vegetarian, when I practically lived on beans, relying on them for protein and to fill me up.

If you have lemon- or herb-infused olive oil on hand—such as that used in the Butterhead Lettuce Salad with Strawberries (page 59)—use it here to add depth to the flavor of this dip. Depending on the potency of your flavored oil, it may be overpowering if used alone, so start with 1 teaspoon and taste it. If you feel the extra flavor it adds is enough, add the remaining 2 teaspoons extra-virgin olive oil.

MAKES ABOUT 3 CUPS

2 19-ounce cans of cannellini or other white beans, rinsed and drained well

1 tablespoon dried red pepper flakes

3 teaspoons extra-virgin olive oil

Kosher salt to taste

Toast Triangles (page 17) or assorted crackers, for serving

1. In a medium serving bowl, place the beans, red pepper flakes, olive oil, and salt to taste. Gently stir to combine.

2. Serve with toast triangles or assorted crackers.

ants on a log

My mother became a special education teacher because my sister Elizabeth was born with a mental disability. Mom was always on the lookout for easy recipes that would allow her to be in the kitchen with all of us. When I told Elizabeth that I was working on a cookbook, she asked if I would include some of her recipes. Of course I said yes right away! Liza is a remarkable person and I love cooking with her. This is a quick and easy snack for kids— although I always catch a few adults sneaking a log or two!

MAKES 16 LOGS

8 stalks celery

½ cup creamy or chunky peanut butter

2 tablespoons raisins

1. Cut the celery sticks crosswise in half. Fill the hollow of each of the 16 celery sticks (the logs) with peanut butter.

2. Stick a few raisins (the ants) in a row on the peanut butter. Serve.

normandy shrimp

The key to this recipe is to use butter from the northern French region of Normandy, or at the very least a European butter, either of which can be found in grocery stores or specialty food shops. Normandy butter contains more fat than American butter and tastes out of this world, especially in a recipe like this one that has just two main ingredients: succulent shrimp and rich butter.

**MAKES 4 TO
6 SERVINGS**

4 tablespoons unsalted Normandy butter

1 pound large (31 to 35 per pound) shrimp, peeled and deveined

2 teaspoons cayenne pepper, or to taste

Pinch of kosher salt

1. In a large skillet over medium heat, melt the butter. Add the shrimp, cayenne, and salt. Cook, gently stirring occasionally and turning the shrimp over at least once, until the shrimp are opaque pink or orange and cooked through, about 6 minutes.

2. Divide the shrimp among 4 to 6 small plates. Pour the remaining butter sauce over each and serve.

ALL ABOUT SHRIMP: SIZING AND COOKING

Where I call for shrimp in this book, you'll see numbers in parentheses after the shrimp weight and size. This recipe, for instance, calls for "1 pound large shrimp (31 to 35 per pound)." The numbers in parentheses are called the "count" and indicate roughly how many shrimp of that size are in 1 pound. Because more general terms such as "small," "medium," "large," and "jumbo" can mean different things depending on where you are, this is a surer indication of what size shrimp I use when I prepare the recipe. It's often marked on the package or at the fish counter as a hyphenated range, such as "31-35." It's fine to use shrimp of a different size if they are all that are available to you; simply adjust the cooking time as necessary.

For recipes that call for cooked shrimp, place the shrimp still in their shells in a large pot of salted water. Bring the water to a boil, then reduce the heat and simmer until the shrimp are pink all over, 2 to 4 minutes for small shrimp and 3 to 5 minutes for large shrimp. Drain and rinse in cold water. When they are cool enough to handle, peel and devein the shrimp. Use or eat at once, or refrigerate until needed or for up to 2 days.

dad's shrimp cocktail

Growing up in the beach town of Corpus Christi, I spent many long hours shrimping, crabbing, and fishing with my dad. I remember my mom frequently asking him, "How on earth am I going to cook all of this?" One way she coped was regular "you-peel-'em" nights, when she would put a couple of enormous bowls of hot, steamed shrimp on the table with many small dishes of Tabasco-infused cocktail sauce. My dad, sisters, and I would happily stay at that table until every bowl was empty.

In Mexico they have their own way of coping with abundant shrimp. No matter where you go, you will find a variation of this traditional appetizer, which is one of my dad's favorite dishes. He loves Tabasco so much that he usually uses double the amount here! Sweet shrimp and velvety avocado temper the heat of the tangy cocktail sauce. Even if you don't like it as spicy as my dad does, it should definitely have a little kick. Mexican shrimp cocktail is typically served out of individual small dishes—I like cocktail glasses—and eaten with a spoon.

MAKES 4 TO 6 SERVINGS

- 1 cup ketchup
- Juice of 2 small lemons (about ¼ cup)
- 1 tablespoon Tabasco sauce
- 1 tablespoon distilled white vinegar
- Kosher salt and ground black pepper to taste
- 1 pound extra small shrimp (61 to 70 per pound), peeled, deveined, cooked (page 25), and cooled
- 4 avocados, pitted, peeled, and cubed
- Lemon wedges, for serving

1. In a small bowl, place the ketchup, lemon juice, Tabasco sauce, vinegar, salt, and pepper. Stir until well blended. In a medium bowl, place the shrimp and avocado. Pour the sauce over and gently toss with a wooden spoon or rubber spatula until the shrimp and avocado are thoroughly coated.

2. Cover and place in the refrigerator for 30 minutes. Divide among 4 to 6 glasses and serve with the lemon wedges.

avocado stuffed with shrimp

As typically Mexican as the previous recipe is, this one is just as typically American, right down to the Miracle Whip, which I have always preferred to mayonnaise. Naturally sweet shrimp is highlighted by a creamy, mildly sweet, tangy dressing and rich, buttery avocado. This is one of my favorite summer appetizers.

MAKES 8 SERVINGS

1 pound small shrimp (51 to 60 per pound), peeled, deveined, cooked (page 25), and chilled

1 medium tomato, seeded and chopped

½ medium white onion, finely chopped

1 to 2 tablespoons chopped fresh cilantro leaves

¼ cup Miracle Whip or mayonnaise

Juice of ½ lime (about 1 tablespoon)

Kosher salt and ground pepper to taste

4 ripe avocados

1. In a large bowl, place the shrimp, tomato, onion, cilantro, Miracle Whip, and lime juice. Stir gently until well mixed. Add salt and pepper to taste.

2. Cut the avocados in half lengthwise and remove the pits. Place one avocado half on each of 8 small plates. Fill each half with a heaping scoop of the shrimp salad and serve.

ceviche

1 pound lump crabmeat

2 pounds small shrimp (51 to 60 per pound), peeled, deveined, cooked (page 25), and chilled

4 ripe avocados, pitted, peeled, and cut into ½-inch dice

4 medium ripe tomatoes, cut into ½-inch dice

2 medium cucumbers, peeled and cut into ½-inch dice

1 large white onion, finely chopped

1 serrano pepper, seeded and finely chopped (optional)

1 bunch of fresh cilantro, leaves chopped

½ to 1 cup Clamato juice

Juice from 3 to 4 limes (6 to 8 tablespoons)

1 teaspoon kosher salt, or to taste

Cholula Hot Sauce to taste (optional)

About 30 tostadas

In the beach towns of Mexico, where fresh seafood is abundant, people happily eat raw fish and shellfish. I, however, do not. I make *ceviche* with cooked shrimp and crab. I do, however, serve my *ceviche* on traditional Mexican tostadas—crispy, fried corn tortillas available at the grocery store.

Use crab that you buy in the refrigerated section of the store. Don't use the shelf-stable crab sold with the canned tuna fish; it doesn't taste nearly as good in this fresh dish. The serrano pepper adds a great, spicy kick, but feel free to leave it out if you prefer. Clamato juice is a combination of tomato and clam juices. It can be found with other cocktail mixers at the grocery store. Cholula hot sauce is made in Mexico; it has a mild flavor and good heat. You'll find it on the same grocery aisle with other hot sauces and condiments.

1. In a large serving bowl, place the crab, shrimp, avocados, tomatoes, cucumbers, onion, serrano (if using), cilantro, Clamato juice, lime juice, salt, and hot sauce (if using). Stir with a fork until gently combined. Cover and refrigerate for 30 minutes.

2. To serve, place the serving bowl out with a stack of tostadas and a large number of small plates so guests can serve themselves.

goat cheese balls

When I first tasted goat cheese, it was definitely not love at first bite. However, when I combined it with two of my favorite ingredients—lemon and Japanese bread crumbs called panko (page 80)—these addictive little morsels were born! These are especially good in place of the crumbled goat cheese on the Baby Spinach with Beets and Goat Cheese (page 55).

The balls are surprisingly easy to make, but they are extremely delicate, so handle them with care. Don't skip the freezer step, which firms them up so they can more easily be breaded and fried, and don't try to handle them with tongs as you might usually do when deep frying. Use a thin, long-handled tool such as a spider (a stainless steel handheld strainer) or slotted spoon. Read about deep-frying on page 37.

MAKES ABOUT 16 BALLS

- 1 11-ounce log soft goat cheese, at room temperature
- ¼ cup fresh Italian parsley leaves, finely chopped
- Grated zest from 2 lemons
- 1 to 2 large eggs
- 1 cup panko
- 2 cups vegetable oil
- Kosher salt to taste

1. In a medium bowl, place the goat cheese, parsley, and lemon zest. Use a fork to break up the cheese and combine the ingredients until well blended.

2. Use your hands to roll into balls about the size of golf balls or a little smaller and place them on a baking sheet. Place in the freezer for 20 minutes.

3. Meanwhile, in a small bowl, beat one egg. Place the panko in a small shallow dish or bowl. Remove the goat cheese balls from the freezer. Coat a goat cheese ball in the egg and then dredge with panko. Transfer to a baking sheet or platter and repeat with the remaining goat cheese balls. Use the remaining egg if necessary.

4. In a large skillet, heat the oil to 350°F. over medium heat. Line a medium baking sheet with paper towels.

5. Gently add several goat cheese balls to the oil and fry until golden brown, 30 to 40 seconds. Gently turn them over and fry until golden brown on the other side, 30 to 40 seconds. Transfer to the paper towel–lined baking sheet and immediately sprinkle lightly with salt. Repeat with the remaining goat cheese balls. Let stand 5 minutes before serving.

tostones

One of my closest girlfriends is from the Caribbean. Every time I go to her house, whether just to gossip over a glass of wine or for a formal sit-down dinner, she puts out a big platter of warm, salty tostones.

For an authentic Caribbean meal, serve these salty, crisp plantains as an appetizer before Crock-Pot Cuban Ropa Vieja (page 113). Be sure that the plantains don't brown the first time you fry them; the goal is just to soften them so they can more easily be flattened into a thinner pancake for the second frying. For more on plantains, see page 153.

MAKES ABOUT 24 CHIPS

4 green plantains

1 cup vegetable oil, or as needed

Kosher salt to taste

FROM AUNT ELSA'S KITCHEN
For the absolute best flavor, sprinkle these with salt as soon as they come out of their second frying and serve hot.

1. Working with one plantain at a time, use a sharp knife to cut off both ends. Run the tip of the knife down the full length of the plantain 2 or 3 times, cutting through the thick skin but not into the plantain. Work the peel off with your hands. Repeat with the remaining plantains.

2. Slice the plantains crosswise into 1-inch thick slices. You should have about 24 pieces.

3. Line a baking sheet with paper towels. In a large skillet, heat the oil over medium heat until hot but not smoking and shimmery.

4. Place the plantains in the oil, seed side down. Cook just until softened, about 4 minutes; do not let them brown. Turn them over and cook the other side. Transfer the pieces to the paper towel–lined baking sheet. Repeat with the remaining pieces.

5. When all of the plantains are cooked and soft, use a tortilla press (page 173) or the bottom of a large can to press each piece into a flattened pancake about ¼ inch thick. Place new paper towels on the baking sheet.

6. Return the pieces to the hot oil and fry until crispy and golden brown, 2 to 3 minutes per side. Less ripe plantains will take longer to cook than riper ones. Transfer to the paper towel–lined pan and immediately sprinkle both sides with salt. When all the tostones are fried, transfer them to a platter and serve hot.

sweet-potato empanadas

Empanadas are a quintessential example of what traditional Latin food is made of: rock-solid and time-tested techniques that can be adapted to accommodate what's available regionally, or in the case of my Aunt Elsa, what was in her pantry. She could pull together the most delicious combinations of ingredients out of what appeared to be thin air and then fill and fry a few dozen pastry wrappers in a flash. When Thanksgiving rolled around, these were our version of the classic American pumpkin pie. Tender, flaky, and lightly sweet, these little "Mexican pumpkin pies" make delicious appetizers, too.

MAKES 30 EMPANADAS

FOR THE DOUGH

4 cups all-purpose flour

¼ cup sugar

1 teaspoon table salt

1¾ cups shortening, at room temperature

1 large egg, lightly beaten

FOR THE FILLING

2 pounds sweet potatoes, peeled and coarsely chopped (or 2 15½-ounce cans sweet potatoes)

2 3-inch cinnamon sticks

¼ to ½ cup sugar, or to taste

1. For the dough: In a large bowl, place the flour, sugar, and salt and whisk together until well blended. Use your hands to knead the shortening into the flour mixture. It will be crumbly and look like coarse meal, and if you squeeze a handful it will cohere but fall apart again when dropped back into the bowl. Add the egg and ½ cup of water, then mix well with a wooden spoon or your hands. Form the dough into a flattened disk, wrap it in plastic wrap, and chill for 1 hour.

2. For the filling: If using fresh sweet potatoes, place them in a large saucepan with the cinnamon sticks and cover with cold water. Simmer, uncovered, until the potatoes are easily pierced with a fork, about 15 minutes. Drain well. Remove and discard the cinnamon sticks. Let stand until cool.

   If using canned sweet potatoes, place them in a large saucepan with their juice. Add the cinnamon sticks and heat over medium heat for about 10 minutes. Remove and discard the cinnamon sticks. Let stand until cool.

3. Transfer the cooled sweet potatoes to the work bowl of a food processor and pulse in one-second bursts just until the potatoes are mashed; do not puree. Stir in the sugar (canned sweet potatoes may already be sweetened).

4. Preheat the oven to 350°F. Line 1 or 2 cookie sheets with parchment paper.

5. Form the dough into 30 golf ball–size balls; keep the balls covered with a damp cloth. On a lightly floured surface, use a rolling pin to roll each ball into a 4-inch circle. Fill each with a scant tablespoon of the mashed sweet potatoes. Fold the dough over the filling to form a half circle and pinch the edges together. Transfer to the prepared baking sheet and cover with a damp cloth. Continue until all the empanadas are formed.

6. Remove the cloth and press the tines of a fork around the edge of each empanada to crimp. Bake until browned, 20 to 25 minutes. Let cool slightly on the baking sheet. Transfer to a platter and serve warm.

DEEP-FRYING

When done correctly, deep-frying produces tender and moist food with a light and crispy exterior. It is not hard to do, especially if you follow just a few important guidelines. To begin, the right tools make the job easier. Invest in a deep-fry thermometer, which is widely available and inexpensive, and takes all the guesswork out of the most important aspect of deep-frying: the temperature of the oil. If you fry in oil that is not hot enough, the food will be soggy; too hot, and the food will burn on the outside before it is cooked on the inside. To use a deep-fry thermometer, simply clip it to the side of the pan so that the bulb of the thermometer is in the oil but not touching the bottom of the pan. Monitor the temperature of the oil throughout the frying process and adjust the heat up or down as necessary to maintain the oil's temperature. Second, use a large, deep pan such as a Dutch oven or a deep, straight-sided skillet. Last, a "spider"—basically a long-handled strainer—or a slotted spoon makes it easy to add and remove food from the hot oil.

A few techniques will help you produce the moist interiors and crispy exteriors that the best deep fryers are known for. First and most important, don't overcrowd the pan. The more cold food you add, the quicker the temperature of the oil will drop and the soggier the end result will be. Fry in batches to maintain a steadier temperature, but make sure the temperature of the oil is returned to the indicated temperature after removing one batch and before adding the next batch. Next, do not skimp on the amount of oil you use. The food you're frying needs room to move around without being crowded. Finally, make sure to remove any large bits of food or coating left in the oil between batches. This can burn and impart flavors to the food you are frying.

argentinean empanadas

These are not the empanadas I grew up with, and until my Argentinean friend Lorena came over one day and made them with me, I would never have considered combining beef with olives and egg whites—but I took one taste and was hooked. Each bite offers an exciting combination of flavors and textures. The secret is that a little cube of Manchego, a Spanish sheep's milk cheese, is nestled into the center of each empanada. When the empanadas are baked or fried, the cheese melts and adds a subtle creaminess, the source of which is elusive to anyone who didn't see you put in the cheese.

Empanada dough disks can be found in the frozen section of many grocery stores or Latin markets. They are made with regular shortening dough or puff pastry; either works beautifully for this recipe. These empanadas are amazing when deep-fried, but they're also really delicious when simply baked; directions for both are below. Read more about deep-frying on page 37.

MAKES 25 TO 30 EMPANADAS

- 2 tablespoons olive oil
- 1 large white onion, chopped
- 2 garlic cloves, minced
- 1½ pounds lean ground beef
- 3 tablespoons paprika
- 2 tablespoons ground cumin
- 1 teaspoon kosher salt or to taste
- ½ teaspoon ground black pepper or to taste
- 2 tablespoons distilled white vinegar
- ¾ cup chopped Spanish green olives stuffed with pimientos

1. In a large skillet, heat the oil over medium heat. Add the onion and garlic and cook until translucent, about 6 minutes. Crumble in the beef, and add the paprika, cumin, salt, and pepper. Cook, stirring frequently, until the beef is browned, about 10 minutes.

2. Drain off the excess grease. Stir in the vinegar. Transfer to a bowl and refrigerate until chilled, about 1 hour. Stir in the olives and hard-cooked egg whites.

3. If baking the empanadas, preheat the oven to 425°F. Coat 2 baking sheets with vegetable oil.

4. When working with empanada disks, always keep all but the disk you're working with covered with a damp towel. If the disks are very firm, place them one at a time on a lightly floured surface and use a rolling pin to roll them to ½ to 1 inch larger than they are to make them a little more pliable.

5. To fill, lay an empanada disk on the work surface. Place about 1½ tablespoons of the meat mixture in the center of the dough disk. Tuck a cube of cheese into the center of the filling. Use your finger to wet the edges of the disk with water and fold over to seal. Gently

3 hard-cooked egg whites, chopped

Vegetable oil, for frying or baking

All-purpose flour, for rolling

25 to 30 store-bought empanada disks, defrosted

25 to 30 ½-inch cubes Manchego cheese

press the tines of a fork along the edge to crimp. Lay the empanada on a baking sheet and cover with a damp towel. Repeat with the remaining filling and dough disks.

6. Brush the tops of the empanadas with vegetable oil and bake until golden brown, 15 to 18 minutes. Serve hot.

If frying the empanadas, fill a skillet ¾ inch deep with vegetable oil and heat to 360°F. over medium heat. Preheat the oven to 200°F. Line 2 baking sheets with paper towels. Fry the empanadas in the oil until golden brown and crisp, 4 to 6 minutes, turning once. Remove with tongs, letting excess oil drip back into the pan, and transfer to a paper towel–lined baking sheet. Keep warm in the oven while you fry the remaining empanadas. Serve hot.

soups & salads

The warm feelings the soups in this chapter evoke in me are not purely physical—although nothing is more warming than a bowl of steaming soup on a cold Texas night (yes, we have them!). I feel so much nostalgia when I prepare and serve these soups, whose delicious aroma and flavor belie how very simple they are to make. That simplicity was absolutely crucial for my mom. With four kids and a husband to feed every day, her approach to food had to be "how quickly can we get something good on the table?" These days my own busy life often puts me in the same frame of mind, and that's when I most appreciate these soups, full of flavor and amazingly quick to pull together. Plus, most can be made vegetarian simply by using vegetable stock in place of the chicken stock—a real plus when I'm serving meat-averse friends.

My favorite salads, the ones I return to again and again, evolved from the trial and error of combining ingredients and flavors I like. Occasionally I would stumble upon a combination that I scribbled on a scrap of paper so that I had a prayer of replicating it! One cardinal truth I've learned over the years is that for green salads, the greens are the key. Tender butterhead lettuce is my absolute favorite, whether dressed simply with extra-virgin olive oil and a little balsamic or in the more layered Butterhead Lettuce Salad with Strawberries (page 59). On the other side of the spectrum is peppery arugula, whose sharp bite is a welcome counterpoint to succulent shrimp in Grilled Shrimp on Arugula (page 52). And in between the two is baby spinach, which I love tossed with Buttermilk Dressing (page 161) or in the perennial favorite, Baby Spinach with Beets and Goat Cheese (page 55).

---

butternut squash soup

tortilla soup

yellow squash soup with lemon

carrot ginger soup

lemon orzo soup

grilled shrimp on arugula

baby spinach with beets and goat cheese

rotini pasta salad

hearts of palm salad

butterhead lettuce salad with strawberries

mexican caprese

corn and zucchini salad

asparagus with grey moss inn white french dressing

butternut squash soup

This soup is as smooth as velvet and has the warm, orange hue of autumn that always looks beautiful in the soup bowl. The cream adds richness, but you can leave it out for a lighter soup that is nonetheless very satisfying.

MAKES 4 TO 6 SERVINGS

- 4 tablespoons (½ stick) unsalted butter
- ½ cup chopped yellow onion
- 2 garlic cloves, minced
- ½ teaspoon kosher salt
- 6 cups peeled and cubed butternut squash (from about a 2-pound squash)
- 5 cups Chicken Broth (page 51), Vegetable Broth (page 49), or store-bought low-sodium chicken broth
- ½ teaspoon chopped fresh thyme leaves (optional)
- ¼ teaspoon ground black pepper
- 1 cup heavy whipping cream (optional)

1. In a Dutch oven or large saucepan over medium heat, melt the butter. Add the onion, garlic, and a pinch of the salt and cook, stirring occasionally, until softened and translucent, about 6 minutes. Add the squash and stir to coat with butter. Cook until softened, about 5 minutes. Add the chicken broth, the thyme (if using), the remaining salt, and the pepper. Bring to a boil. Reduce the heat and simmer, partially covered, until the squash is very tender, about 12 minutes.

2. Transfer the soup in batches to the work bowl of a food processor and puree until very smooth.

3. Return the soup to the pot and stir in the cream, if using. Taste and adjust the seasoning.

4. Heat through, but do not allow the soup to boil or the cream may curdle. Ladle the soup into 4 to 6 soup bowls and serve hot.

FROM AUNT ELSA'S KITCHEN
As long as their skin is free of any cuts, butternut squash and other winter squash will last for two to three months stored in a cool, dry place. So the next time you see them at the farmer's market, stock up!

tortilla soup

My friends request this recipe more often than any other. I am often asked if it's a family recipe. I take it as a compliment that people always seem so surprised to hear that I found it in a magazine when I was about twelve years old. I've made it so many times since then and it has evolved into what it is today. I think it's so delicious—and popular!—because of its clear but very flavorful broth. So often tortilla soup is heavy, but this one is hearty without being unpleasantly thick.

In fact, I make such a large batch because everyone always wants seconds and thirds. On the rare occasions that I've had leftovers, I've discovered that the soup keeps very well, and even gets better, stored in a tightly covered container in the refrigerator. The garnishes keep well stored in zip-top bags; keep the fried tortilla strips at room temperature and everything else in the refrigerator. When serving the second day, just place all the garnishes at the bottom of the bowl and ladle the soup over.

I use two kinds of dried chiles—ancho and pasilla—because they add more depth and smoky notes to the broth. Use more or fewer chiles depending on how strong you want their flavor to be. For more on dried chiles, see page 96.

MAKES 14 TO 16 SERVINGS

- 4 pounds chicken legs
- 4 pounds chicken thighs
- 12 cups Chicken Broth (page 51), store-bought low-sodium chicken broth, or cold water
- 4 dried pasilla chiles
- 4 dried ancho chiles
- 6 tomatoes, chopped
- 1 large white onion, diced
- 6 large garlic cloves, peeled
- 2 teaspoons kosher salt, or to taste
- 2 large bunches of fresh cilantro, leaves chopped

1. In a large stockpot, place the chicken legs and thighs and the broth or cold water. Bring to a boil over medium-high heat. Reduce the heat and simmer until the chicken is opaque throughout and tender when pierced with a fork, about 30 minutes. With a slotted spoon remove the chicken from the pot and set aside to cool. Set aside the stockpot of broth. As soon as the chicken is cool enough to handle, pull off and shred the meat; discard the skin and bones.

2. Meanwhile, place the pasilla and ancho chiles in a medium saucepan and add cold water to cover. Bring the water to a boil over medium heat. Reduce the heat and simmer until the chiles are soft, about 10 minutes. Drain the chiles and remove their stems and veins. If you want a spicier bite, keep the seeds; if not, remove the seeds as well.

3. In the work bowl of a food processor, place the chiles, tomatoes, onion, garlic, and the salt. Process until smooth, adding a ½ cup of the reserved chicken broth to loosen the mixture if it is too thick.

(recipe continues)

1 cup vegetable oil, plus
   more if needed

36 white or yellow corn
    tortillas, sliced into
    ¼-inch-thick strips

1 head iceberg lettuce,
   cored and shredded

6 large avocados, pitted,
   peeled, and diced

3 cups grated or
   crumbled queso fresco
   (about 12 ounces)

4. Stir the chile puree and half of the cilantro into the broth. Bring to a simmer over low heat, and simmer for 20 to 30 minutes. Taste and add salt if needed. Stir in the reserved chicken and the remaining cilantro and remove the pot from the heat.

5. While the broth is simmering, line a baking sheet or large plate with paper towels. In a large skillet, heat the oil over medium-high heat until hot but not smoking and shimmery. Add a handful or two of tortilla strips—they can be touching but not overlapping—and fry just until lightly browned around the edges, about 45 seconds. Use tongs or a spider to transfer the strips to the paper towels, tossing and moving them around so they take on squiggly shapes as they cool and harden. Continue in batches until all the tortilla strips are fried, adding more oil to the pan if necessary.

6. When ready to serve, place the lettuce, avocado, and queso fresco in separate bowls to make serving easier.

7. For each serving, place a few tortillas strips and a scoop of lettuce in a soup bowl. Ladle the soup into the bowl. Top with a spoonful of avocado, sprinkle some queso fresco on top, and serve.

yellow squash soup with lemon

When I was a kid we grew all our own vegetables, especially *calabasa,* or squash. LOTS of squash. To be honest, I got a little sick of it (don't worry—my mom already knows). Then I grew up and figured out a few surefire ways to show off the delicious earthiness and sweetness of summer squash. This soup is one of them; the lemon gives it great tang and the soup is unexpectedly creamy, even though there's not a bit of cream or milk in it.

Be sure to puree this soup in batches—don't pour the soup over the level of the top of the food processor blade. This soup is brothy before it's pureed, and it'll seep out of the work bowl and all over the counter if you're not careful.

MAKES 6 TO 8 SERVINGS

- 3 tablespoons extra-virgin olive oil
- 3 medium leeks (white and light green parts), finely chopped
- 2 medium yellow onions, finely chopped
- 6 garlic cloves, minced

  Kosher salt to taste
- 6 medium yellow squash, coarsely chopped
- 4 sprigs of fresh thyme
- 6 cups Chicken Broth (page 51), Vegetable Broth (page 49), or store-bought low-sodium chicken broth

  Juice of 1 small lemon (about 2 tablespoons), or to taste

1. In a large soup pot or Dutch oven, heat the oil over medium heat. Stir in the leeks, onions, garlic, and a pinch of salt and cook, stirring occasionally, until the onions are translucent, about 6 minutes. Add the squash and thyme and cook, stirring occasionally, until the squash begins to soften, 5 to 10 minutes. Add the chicken broth and increase the heat to high. Bring to a boil and boil gently for 5 minutes. Reduce the heat and simmer, covered, until the vegetables are very tender, about 20 minutes.

2. Remove and discard the thyme sprigs. Transfer the soup in 3 or more batches to the work bowl of a food processor and puree until smooth. Pour the soup back into the soup pot and reheat over medium heat until hot. Stir in the lemon juice and salt to taste. Ladle into 6 to 8 soup bowls and serve.

FROM AUNT ELSA'S KITCHEN

Tie the thyme sprigs together with kitchen string so you can just pluck the bundle out after the soup is cooked.

carrot ginger soup

I love the refreshing flavor and heat of fresh ginger and this soup shows it off beautifully, especially if you use the full three tablespoons of ginger listed below. It even causes a pleasant burn in the back of your throat. If you prefer a little less assertiveness, use just two tablespoons. Either way, keep in mind that ginger becomes more pronounced over time, so although the soup stores very well, the ginger's bite will become stronger.

Many recipes for carrot and other pureed vegetable soups call for toppings of one kind or another, but I really prefer to let the natural flavors of the soup and veggies shine through, so I skip them. You can always top with a scattering of whatever fresh herb is in the soup, though, which is very pretty and highlights the flavors already in the soup. Be sure to cook the carrots until they are very tender so that they'll puree to a silky smooth soup.

MAKES 4 TO 6 SERVINGS

3 tablespoons unsalted butter

1 large yellow onion, chopped

6 garlic cloves, minced

Kosher salt

2 pounds carrots, chopped

2 to 3 tablespoons peeled and chopped fresh ginger

5 cups Vegetable Broth (recipe follows) or store-bought low-sodium vegetable broth

2 sprigs of fresh thyme, plus fresh leaves for serving, if desired

1 fresh or dried bay leaf

Ground black pepper to taste

½ cup whole milk

1. In a large soup pot over medium heat, melt the butter. Add the onion, garlic, and a pinch of salt, and cook, stirring occasionally, until the onion is translucent, about 6 minutes. Stir in the carrots and ginger and cook, stirring occasionally, for 5 minutes. Stir in the vegetable broth, thyme, bay leaf, and a few grindings of black pepper. Increase the heat to high. Bring to a boil and adjust the heat to boil gently for 5 minutes. Reduce the heat and simmer, partially covered, until the carrots are very soft, 20 to 25 minutes.

2. Remove and discard the thyme sprigs and bay leaf. Transfer the soup in batches to the work bowl of a food processor and puree until very smooth. Pour the soup back into the soup pot and reheat over medium heat until hot. Stir in the milk. Season with salt and pepper to taste. Ladle the soup into 4 to 6 soup bowls and garnish with thyme leaves, if desired. Serve hot.

FROM AUNT ELSA'S KITCHEN

The most time-consuming part of this and the Butternut Squash Soup (page 43) is the chopping. You can buy the carrots or squash already chopped in many stores, but they're ridiculously expensive. To get ahead for the busy week without breaking the bank, spend a little time over the weekend peeling and chopping carrots and winter squash by hand or, even faster, by pulsing in the food processor. Place the chopped vegetables in a zip-top freezer bag and freeze until needed. The soups come together in no time when the chopping is done ahead.

vegetable broth

MAKES ABOUT 8 CUPS

- 2 medium yellow onions, each cut into 8 wedges

- 3 carrots, coarsely chopped

- 2 ribs celery, coarsely chopped

- 1 leek (white and light green parts), coarsely chopped

- 4 sprigs of fresh parsley

- 4 sprigs of fresh thyme

- 1 fresh or dried bay leaf

- ¼ teaspoon whole black peppercorns

1. In a large stockpot, place the onions, carrots, celery, leek, parsley, thyme, bay leaf, peppercorns, and 12 cups of water. Bring to a boil over medium-high heat. Reduce the heat and simmer, uncovered, until the broth is flavorful, 30 to 45 minutes.

2. Strain the broth through a mesh strainer and discard the solids; do not press on the vegetables while straining or the broth will turn cloudy. Let cool.

3. Store in tightly covered containers in the refrigerator for up to 5 days or freeze up to 6 months.

lemon orzo soup

This soup can be pulled together in minutes, and it's one of the most soul-satisfying things I make. It should be very brothy so the orzo just floats in the rich, lemony broth. The pasta will absorb the broth as it sits, so serve as soon as it's ready.

SERVES 2 TO 4

4 to 5 cups Chicken Broth (recipe follows), Vegetable Broth (page 49), or store-bought low-sodium chicken broth, or as needed

1 cup dried orzo pasta

Juice from 1 to 2 small lemons (2 to 4 tablespoons juice)

2 large egg yolks

Pinch of kosher salt

1. In a small saucepan, bring the chicken broth to a boil. Stir in the orzo and cook until al dente, 8 to 9 minutes. The soup should be very brothy. Add more hot stock if necessary. Stir in the lemon juice.

2. In a small bowl, beat the egg yolks. Stir the hot broth into the egg yolks 1 tablespoon at a time, up to 6 tablespoons. This tempers the yolks and prevents them from cooking too fast and curdling. Stir the yolks into the soup. Add a pinch of salt, or to taste. Ladle the soup into 2 to 4 soup bowls and serve at once.

chicken broth

MAKES ABOUT 4 QUARTS

1 tablespoon vegetable oil

3 pounds chicken wings

1 medium yellow onion, cut into eight wedges

1 carrot, chopped

1 celery rib, chopped

4 sprigs of fresh parsley

3 sprigs of fresh thyme

½ teaspoon whole black peppercorns

2 fresh or dried bay leaves

1. In a large stockpot, heat the oil over medium heat. Add the chicken wings, onion, carrot, and celery and cook, stirring, until the vegetables are softened, about 10 minutes; do not let the chicken brown.

2. Add cold water to cover the ingredients by 2 inches. Bring to a boil over high heat. Use a large spoon to skim off any foam that rises to the surface. Add the parsley, thyme, peppercorns, and bay leaves. Reduce the heat to low and simmer, partially covered, until the broth is full flavored, 2 to 3 hours. Strain the broth through a mesh strainer and discard the solids. Let cool.

3. If desired, refrigerate the stock and remove and discard the solidified fat from the surface. Store in tightly covered containers in the refrigerator for up to 5 days or freeze up to 6 months.

grilled shrimp on arugula

FOR THE SHRIMP

4 tablespoons olive oil

Juice of 3 small lemons (about 6 tablespoons juice)

4 garlic cloves, minced

2 teaspoons chopped fresh oregano

2 teaspoons chopped fresh basil

2 teaspoons chopped fresh chives

Pinch of ground cayenne or to taste

Kosher salt and ground black pepper to taste

24 jumbo shrimp (21 to 25 per pound), peeled and deveined but with the tails on

FOR THE SALAD

4 ounces green beans, trimmed and cut into 2-inch pieces

2 10-ounce bags baby arugula leaves

1 pint small grape tomatoes, or halved if large

2 tablespoons extra-virgin olive oil

2 tablespoons white balsamic vinegar

Kosher salt and ground black pepper to taste

This marinade is my favorite for shrimp, chicken, and flank steak or any other red meat. As with any marinade, the longer you let the shrimp or meat marinate, the better, but on many occasions I've had only enough time to throw it together and put it straight on the grill, and the results are still great.

1. In a large bowl, place the olive oil, lemon juice, garlic, oregano, basil, chives, cayenne, salt, and pepper. Stir until well blended. Add the shrimp and stir gently until well coated with marinade. Cover and refrigerate for 2 hours.

2. Prepare a medium bowl of ice water. Bring a small saucepan of lightly salted water to a boil. Add the green beans and cook until crisp-tender, about 3 minutes. Drain the beans and immediately add to the ice water. Let stand until cool. Drain well and set aside.

3. When ready to serve, prepare a medium-hot grill or set a rack 6 inches from the broiler and set the broiler to high. Grill or broil the shrimp until they are firm and bright pink or orange, 4 to 5 minutes, turning once during cooking.

4. In a large salad bowl, place the arugula, tomatoes, reserved green beans, oil, vinegar, salt, and pepper. Toss gently until the arugula and vegetables are well coated.

5. Divide the greens among 4 to 6 salad plates and top with the shrimp. Serve.

baby spinach with beets and goat cheese

For as long as I can remember I've been awed by the almost jewel-like beauty of beets. When I was a kid I longed for a crayon that was the exact color of the beets we grew on the ranch so I could use it in all my drawings. I think this is why my mother never had any trouble getting me to eat them! I love beets in salads or on their own, simply drizzled with extra-virgin olive oil and a little fresh lemon juice.

MAKES 4 SERVINGS

1 5-ounce bag baby spinach

2 tablespoons Balsamic Vinaigrette (page 159) or to taste

1 bunch of beets, roasted or boiled (see box), peeled and thinly sliced

½ cup crumbled goat cheese

1. Place the baby spinach in a salad bowl. Add the balsamic vinaigrette and toss gently until well coated.

2. Divide the spinach among 4 shallow bowls or salad plates. Top with the beet slices and sprinkle over the crumbled goat cheese. Serve.

COOKING BEETS

To prepare the beets, trim all but about 1 inch of the stems. Rinse thoroughly under cold, running water.

To boil beets, bring a large saucepan of water to a boil. Add the beets and return the water to a boil. Reduce the heat and simmer, covered, until the beets are tender when pierced with a thin, sharp knife, about 20 minutes for small beets, about 30 minutes for medium beets, and 45 minutes to 1 hour for large beets. Drain the beets and transfer them to a bowl of ice water until cool enough to handle.

To bake beets, preheat the oven to 400°F. Place the beets in a small roasting pan and add ½ cup of water. Seal the pan tightly with foil and bake until the beets are tender when pierced with a thin, sharp knife, about 45 minutes for small beets, about 1 hour for medium beets, and about 1¼ hours for large beets (be careful when lifting the foil; don't get burned by the escaping hot steam). Remove the beets from the pan and let stand. When the beets are cool enough to handle, use a paring knife to trim the ends and slip off their skins. Serve warm, at room temperature, or cold.

FROM AUNT ELSA'S KITCHEN

Beets retain better flavor when they are boiled or baked with their skins on, but peeling them after cooking can transfer all that beautiful color right to your hands, where it doesn't look so nice. Wear kitchen gloves when peeling and chopping beets.

rotini pasta salad

Full of colorful, crunchy vegetables and bursting with flavor, this looks really pretty on a buffet table. By the time I was in middle school, I knew that rotini and vegetables in the kitchen was the sign that we were headed to a potluck soon. This was and is my mom's go-to recipe for PTA meetings, school plays, recitals, and baby and bridal showers.

MAKES 6 SERVINGS

- 1 pound dried rotini or farfalle
- 1 to 2 tablespoons extra-virgin olive oil (optional)
- 1 pint cherry or grape tomatoes
- ½ large red onion, thinly sliced
- 1 green bell pepper, cored, seeded, and coarsely chopped
- 1 4-ounce can sliced mushrooms, well drained
- 2 teaspoons dry salad seasoning
- ½ cup Balsamic Vinaigrette (page 159) or bottled Italian salad dressing
- ¼ cup grated Parmesan cheese, or to taste

1. Bring a large pot of salted water to a boil over high heat. Stir in the pasta and cook until al dente, about 8 minutes or according to the package directions. Drain the pasta and rinse with cold water to stop the cooking. Drain very well and transfer to a large mixing bowl. If the pasta will need to sit on its own for a little while, add 1 to 2 tablespoons olive oil, if desired, to prevent sticking, and toss to coat.

2. Place the pasta in a large bowl. Add the tomatoes, red onion, bell pepper, mushrooms, salad seasoning, and dressing.

3. Toss gently until well mixed and coated with dressing. Sprinkle over the Parmesan cheese and serve.

hearts of palm salad

Café Med in Los Angeles serves a salad like this over paper-thin beef carpaccio that I love to order because it's so light and fresh. When I make it at home, I skip the beef but pile on the greens.

MAKES 4 SERVINGS

1 10-ounce bag fresh arugula

¼ cup Lemon Garlic Dressing (page 159)

Kosher salt and ground black pepper

1 14-ounce can artichoke hearts, drained and quartered

1 14-ounce can hearts of palm, drained and sliced

Shaved Parmigiano-Reggiano cheese

1. Place the arugula in a large serving bowl. Pour over the dressing and toss gently to coat. Add salt and pepper to taste.

2. Scatter the artichoke hearts and hearts of palm on top. Use a vegetable peeler to shave the Parmigiano-Reggiano on top. Serve.

PAPER OR PLASTIC?

When the checkout person at the supermarket asks, in regard to your bag choice, "Paper or plastic?" the best answer is, "Neither, thanks!" Paper is not much better than plastic. Even though paper bags are easy to recycle in many areas, it actually takes enormous resources to manufacture them. Please invest in a few reusable shopping and produce bags (yes, they make these, too!) and bring them with you to the store. They can last for years, which, if you consider how many bags' worth of groceries you buy each week, can really add up!

butterhead lettuce salad with strawberries

Usually when I make a salad, I start with a base of greens—most often tender butterhead lettuce, my favorite—dress it with a flavorful vinaigrette, and then top it with whatever I have on hand. The combination in this recipe was one I tried once and loved so much that it's become a staple at my house.

MAKES 4 SERVINGS

- 1 small head butterhead lettuce, washed and dried
- 2 tablespoons lemon-flavored olive oil
- 2 tablespoons balsamic vinegar
- ½ small green apple, cored and very thinly sliced
- 1 pint strawberries, hulled and thinly sliced (about 2 cups)
- ½ cup walnuts, coarsely chopped
- ¼ cup crumbled goat cheese

1. Tear the lettuce leaves into pieces slightly larger than bite size. Place them in a large salad bowl. Pour over the oil and vinegar and toss gently until well coated.

2. Arrange the apples, strawberries, and walnuts on top of the lettuce. Sprinkle the crumbled goat cheese on top and serve.

mexican caprese

My version of the classic Insalata Caprese—an Italian salad of mozzarella, tomatoes, and basil—uses green avocados in place of the basil for a Mexican twist. I like to say that the red, white, and green represent the Mexican flag! I arrange this on a big serving platter and place it right in the middle of the dinner table or a buffet—it's visually arresting and really makes the table pop beautifully.

MAKES 6 TO 8 SERVINGS

2 red tomatoes, flavorful heirlooms if possible, cored and sliced

1 pound fresh mozzarella, sliced

3 avocados, pitted, peeled, and sliced

Good-quality balsamic vinegar to taste

1. On a large serving platter, arrange the tomatoes, mozzarella, and avocados in an overlapping and repeating pattern.

2. Drizzle with vinegar and serve.

CHOOSING AND PREPARING AVOCADOS

Use properly ripe avocados, which should be firm but give a bit when pressed gently. If they don't give at all, they're underripe. To ripen avocados at home, place them in a brown paper bag and store them at room temperature. They'll usually ripen in a couple of days, but some can take up to five days. I always buy local, organic avocados in Texas and California, and I recommend that you do the same when possible.

A ripe avocado can be tricky to slice or dice neatly. By the time you've scooped it out of the shell, bits of the soft inside are often left behind and the avocado can look manhandled. Instead, remove the pit and use a small, thin-bladed knife to slice or dice one half at a time right in the shell. Use a spoon to gently scoop out the sliced or diced avocado.

corn and zucchini salad

I love learning new things every time I eat a dish or step into a kitchen or take a cooking class. I was thrilled to discover Maite Gomez-Rejón's program in Los Angeles called ArtBites, which combines art history and the culinary arts in classes that begin with viewing a collection at a local museum and end in the kitchen. I took a class called "Dining in the Aztec Empire," in which Maite taught us modern ways to use ingredients that would have been used in what is now central Mexico during the fourteenth through sixteenth centuries. I learned this recipe, which uses the ancient ingredients corn and squash, in that wonderful class.

MAKES 6 TO 8 SERVINGS

- 5 ears of corn, shucked
- 1 tablespoon unsalted butter
- 2 cups ¼-inch diced zucchini
- ½ teaspoon kosher salt
- ¼ cup finely chopped red onion
- 1½ tablespoons apple cider vinegar
- 2 tablespoons extra-virgin olive oil
- ½ teaspoon ground black pepper
- ½ cup chopped fresh cilantro or basil

1. Prepare a large bowl of ice water and set aside. Bring a large pot of water to a boil. Add the corn to the boiling water, cover, and remove from the heat. Let stand 3 to 5 minutes. Drain and immerse the corn in the ice water to stop the cooking. When cool, cut the kernels off the cob, cutting close to the cob. Place the kernels in a large bowl.

2. In a small skillet over medium heat, melt the butter. Add the zucchini and a pinch of salt and cook, stirring, until tender, about 4 minutes. Add the zucchini to the bowl with the corn.

3. Add to the bowl the red onion, vinegar, oil, remaining salt, and pepper. Just before serving, toss in the herbs. Taste, adjust the seasoning as needed, and serve cold or at room temperature.

FROM AUNT ELSA'S KITCHEN
To quickly and easily get the silk off an ear of corn, use a dry paper towel to brush downward on the cob.

asparagus with grey moss inn white french dressing

Reading through this book, you may pick up on a theme: I hide nutritious vegetables under generous amounts of sauce or cheese so everyone will eat them. Here is an example of my fun cat-and-mouse game played to perfection: creamy, oniony dressing is lapped over crisp-tender asparagus—and everyone's happy!

MAKES 4 SERVINGS

1 pound asparagus, ends trimmed

¼ cup Grey Moss Inn White French Dressing (page 160), or to taste

1. Prepare a bowl of ice water and set aside. In a sauté pan with a tight-fitting lid, add water to about ½ inch deep. Bring to a boil. Add the asparagus and simmer until bright green and just tender when pierced with a thin, sharp knife, 2 to 4 minutes.

2. Drain the asparagus and immediately plunge into the ice water to stop the cooking. When cool, drain the asparagus and lay them out on a clean kitchen towel. Transfer to a large serving platter. Drizzle the dressing over the asparagus and serve.

fish main courses

A childhood spent on the water meant that by the time I was seven years old, I could catch, gut, and fillet a fish. This is an undeniably useful skill, although I'm no longer frequently called upon to use it in my day job, and it instilled in me a deep and abiding respect for all sea life. Today when I buy and prepare fish, I seek out the highest quality, most sustainably caught fish I can find. I love a culinary challenge, and over the years I've developed a few foolproof cooking methods for fish. I've also discovered that adding favorite ingredients, such as honey and citrus, is a surefire way to make any fish taste great.

When buying fish, choose fresh, not frozen. To choose the most sustainably caught fish and shellfish, check out the Monterey Bay Aquarium's Seafood Watch (see Resources, page 220) for a user-friendly, regularly updated list of how fish and shellfish are being caught or raised. You can consult the online database, download a smartphone application, or carry the really useful pocket guides that indicate which are "best choices" and "good alternatives," and which you should avoid. They believe, as I do, that the choices we make as individuals absolutely make a difference in our world.

crispy and spicy catfish fillets

lemon dover sole

honey-glazed salmon

tilapia with citrus-garlic sauce

herbed sea bass in parchment

crispy and spicy catfish fillets

When I went fishing with my dad, more often than not we caught buckets of catfish. I loved every moment of those days, right up until he'd cook the catfish by just tossing it on the grill with nothing more than some salt and pepper—then I wasn't so happy. I loved just about anything breaded—still do!—so I took matters into my own hands and came up with this recipe (see photograph on page 66). The breading keeps the fish tender and moist. The only thing I've changed about this dish since I was a kid is the bread crumbs. Ever since fluffy Japanese panko (page 80) has become widely available, I use it instead of regular dried bread crumbs for almost all my breaded dishes. Try this with Spicy Roasted Brussels Sprouts (page 138) and Lemon Fettuccine (page 134).

MAKES 8 SERVINGS

Vegetable oil spray

1 large egg

½ cup buttermilk

2 to 3 cups panko

8 5- to 6-ounce catfish fillets

1 tablespoon Old Bay or Season-All seasoning

1 to 2 lemons, sliced, for serving

1. Position a rack in the top third of the oven and preheat the oven to 400°F. Coat a large baking sheet with vegetable oil spray.

2. In a wide, shallow bowl, whisk together the egg and buttermilk. Place the panko in another wide, shallow dish. Sprinkle the fillets all over with the Old Bay seasoning.

3. Working with one fillet at a time, coat it on both sides with the egg mixture and allow the excess to drip off. Place it in the panko, and coat on both sides. Transfer to the prepared baking sheet. Repeat with the remaining fillets, arranging them on the baking sheet in a staggered formation so they all fit. Spray the fillets with the vegetable oil.

4. Bake for 8 minutes. Use a spatula to carefully flip the fillets and spray them again with oil. Bake until lightly browned, about 8 minutes more. Serve with lemon slices.

lemon dover sole

While in the port town of Fécamp in Normandy, France, I stopped for lunch at a tiny hotel-restaurant that had no more than four tables and was run by a husband-and-wife team who apparently did everything from the cooking to serving to making the beds themselves. The catch of the day was Dover sole and the chef served it lightly pan-fried and practically swimming in a bath of the most wonderful lemon-butter sauce I'd ever tasted. The Dover sole sold in Europe is a delicate flat fish native to European waters, including the English Channel on which the town of Fécamp sits. When I'm in the United States, I use Pacific Dover sole or another delicately flavored, fresh, flat fish from waters closer to home. This dish is excellent served with Broiled Asparagus (page 145).

MAKES 6 SERVINGS

3 pounds flat fish, such as flounder, halibut, or sand dab

½ teaspoon kosher salt

2 tablespoons olive oil, or as needed

Ingredients for Lemon Butter Sauce (page 166, see Note)

NOTE
The best time to prepare the sauce is indicated in the recipe.

1. Lightly sprinkle both sides of the fillets with salt. In a large skillet, heat the oil over medium heat. Add as many fillets to the skillet as will fit without crowding. Cook until lightly browned on the bottom, 3 to 4 minutes. Turn and cook until done, 3 to 4 minutes.

2. Remove to a platter, keeping the fish warm, and continue with the remaining fillets, adding more oil to the pan if needed.

3. Prepare the lemon butter sauce.

4. Divide the fillets among 6 plates, pour the lemon sauce over the fish, and serve.

honey-glazed salmon

To be honest, I didn't used to care for salmon. I tried a number of different methods of cooking it and none had ever worked for me. Then, finally, I asked my friend Mario Lopez for advice, and he responded with two words: "honey glaze." That was it! Honey cuts the richness that I used to find overpowering while underscoring the salmon's own sweetness.

Baking the fish in paper packages, called *en papillote* in French, allows thicker cuts to cook all the way through without getting dry, and (better yet) keeps the mess to a minimum. Plus, it's fun to open them at the table—just be careful not to get burned by the steam! Serve with Garlic Green Beans (page 141) or a green salad.

MAKES 4 SERVINGS

- 3 tablespoons honey
- 2 tablespoons olive oil
- Juice from 1 small lemon (about 2 tablespoons)
- 3 garlic cloves, minced
- Parchment paper
- 4 6-ounce boneless salmon fillets, about 1½-inch thick
- Kosher salt and ground black pepper to taste

1. Preheat the oven to 450°F.

2. In a small bowl, place the honey, oil, lemon juice, and garlic. Stir until well blended.

3. Cut four 15-inch squares of parchment. Lay a fillet skin side down just below the center of one parchment square. Generously brush it with the honey glaze. Sprinkle with salt and pepper.

4. Fold the top half of the parchment down so that the edges meet. Fold the three open sides several times to create tightly sealed "pouches." Place the packet on a baking sheet and repeat with the remaining fillets. Bake until cooked, 12 to 15 minutes depending on the fillets' thickness and how rare you want the fish. Remember that the fish will continue to cook a little more after it's removed from the oven. Transfer a package to each of 4 plates and serve.

tilapia with citrus-garlic sauce

I don't understand why tilapia is not more popular. It has a flaky texture and good and delicate flavor and can be cooked just about any way you'd prepare any other fish. Plus, it's safely and sustainably fished, widely available, and affordable. I buy and cook quite a bit of it, sometimes because I seek it out specifically, as when I make this recipe. Other times I get it because I request a specific fish and am told that it's frozen in the back of the store. In these cases, I choose tilapia instead and am never disappointed.

MAKES 4 SERVINGS

4   5- to 6-ounce tilapia
     fillets

     Kosher salt to taste

1   tablespoon olive oil

     Ingredients for Citrus-
     Garlic Sauce (page
     165, see Note)

NOTE
The best time to prepare the sauce is indicated in the recipe.

1. Sprinkle the fillets on both sides with salt. In a large skillet, heat the oil over medium heat until it's hot but not smoking. Add the tilapia to the pan and cook until the fish is opaque, about 3 minutes per side. Remove from the pan and keep warm.

2. Wipe out the skillet and prepare the citrus-garlic sauce. Arrange the fillets on 4 individual plates or on a platter. Pour the sauce over the fillets and serve.

herbed sea bass in parchment

As useful as the paper package method is to cook thicker cuts of rich fish (see Honey-Glazed Salmon, page 73) it is also great for delicate, flaky white fish that can be difficult to handle during cooking and dries out easily.

MAKES 4 SERVINGS

Parchment paper

4 6-ounce sea bass or striped bass fillets

Kosher salt and ground black pepper to taste

8 sprigs of fresh lemon thyme or thyme

3 tablespoons unsalted butter, divided into 4 equal pieces

1. Preheat the oven to 450°F.

2. Cut four 15-inch squares of parchment. Lay a fillet just below the center of one parchment square. Sprinkle with salt and pepper, and lay 2 lemon thyme sprigs and a pat of butter on top.

3. Fold the top half of the parchment down so that the edges meet. Fold the three open sides several times to create tightly sealed "pouches." Place the packet on a baking sheet and repeat with the remaining fillets. Bake until just cooked through, 10 to 12 minutes, depending on the fillets' thickness. Remember that the fish will continue to cook a little more after it's removed from the oven. Transfer a package to each of 4 plates and serve.

poultry main courses

Like children everywhere, many kids at my school had pet dogs and cats. I had chickens. Every day I let them out of the coop to peck at bugs and the feed I scattered and every evening I had to corral them back into the coop, a chore akin to herding fifty kittens. I collected their eggs every day, except those that we left to hatch, and then I held and petted and whispered to the precious baby chicks. Looking back, I smile to think that when I was very young, I made no connection between these pecking, clucking little friends of mine and the chicken my mom bought at the market every week (we never ate our chickens . . . or at least no one ever told me we did). Of course I'm wiser now, and the time I spent with those chickens taught me to treat the creatures we raise for food with the dignity and respect every living being deserves. Because of this, when I buy poultry and eggs, I'm careful about my choices (page 79).

Once you have your chicken or turkey in hand, turn to the recipes in this chapter for crowd-pleasers of every type. There's fun finger food that can also make a meal, such as Chicken Salad Sandwiches (page 88) and BBQ Chicken Pizza (page 91); hearty stews and casseroles like Hungarian Paprika Chicken (page 84) and Hot Chicken Salad (page 79); and favorites that I turn to again and again, including Lemon Fried Chicken (page 80) and Chicken with Caramelized Shallots and Shiitake-Wine Sauce (page 83). Enjoy!

---

hot chicken salad

lemon fried chicken

chicken with caramelized shallots and shiitake-wine sauce

hungarian paprika chicken

chalupas

chicken salad sandwiches

bbq chicken pizza

flautas

enchiladas rojas (red enchiladas)

turkey shepherd's pie

hot chicken salad

When I am in Malibu, I often serve this cheesy, hearty dish with a fresh fruit salad and warm croissants for brunch on the veranda.

MAKES 4 TO 6 SERVINGS

Vegetable oil or cooking spray, for the baking dish

4 cups cooked, diced chicken (page 89)

1 cup sliced almonds

1 8-ounce can artichoke hearts, drained and chopped

½ cup diced celery

3 green onions (white and light green parts), chopped

4 teaspoons fresh lemon juice

1 8-ounce package shredded Colby and Monterey Jack Cheese (about 2 cups)

½ teaspoon kosher salt

½ teaspoon ground black pepper

1 cup mayonnaise

1½ cups salted potato chips, crushed

1. Preheat the oven to 375°F. Lightly spray or coat a 2-quart baking dish with vegetable oil.

2. In a large mixing bowl, place the chicken, almonds, artichoke hearts, celery, green onion, lemon juice, cheese, salt, and pepper. Stir until well combined. Add the mayonnaise and stir until well coated.

3. Transfer the mixture to the prepared baking dish and scatter the crushed potato chips over the surface of the dish. Bake until the cheese is melted and the top is lightly browned, about 30 minutes. Let stand 5 to 10 minutes before serving.

ORGANIC POULTRY AND EGGS

When I buy poultry and eggs at the grocery store, I generally choose organic. Unlike "free-range," which means only that the producer must allow the chickens access to the outdoors (it doesn't matter if that's an asphalt lot), the term "organic" is strictly regulated by the U.S. Department of Agriculture. When shopping at a farmer's market, I tend to worry less about the labels. Many smaller farmers can't afford the time and money that strict federal regulations require, so even though they follow all the standards, they may not have the label. Check out localharvest.org to find reputable farmers near you who are raising animals in a humane and healthy way. Just type in your zip code to locate nearby farmers' markets and grocery stores where you can find sustainable and organic produce, poultry, meat, and eggs.

lemon fried chicken

Ever since I discovered panko (see box), I make this easy dish all the time. The trick is to work fast once the chicken is cooked and add the salt and lemon as soon as you get the chicken out of the pan. Don't worry if it looks like too much lemon juice—when the chicken is hot, the juice soaks through the crispy coating and adds fabulous flavor to the chicken.

MAKES 6 TO 8 SERVINGS

2 1¼-pound packages thinly sliced chicken breasts

4 large eggs

3 to 4 cups panko

1 cup vegetable oil or as needed

Kosher salt to taste

3 lemons, halved

1. Rinse and pat dry the chicken breasts. Lay them on a work surface between two layers of plastic wrap. Gently pound with a meat tenderizer until they are about ⅛ inch thick.

2. In a large, shallow dish, beat the eggs. Pour the panko in another large, shallow dish. Working with one piece at a time, coat the chicken on both sides with egg. Let the excess run off and then dredge both sides in the panko. Place the chicken on a large baking sheet or platter and continue with the remaining chicken.

3. Line 1 or 2 large platters or baking sheets with paper towels. In a large skillet over medium-high heat, heat the oil until shimmery and hot but not smoking. Place as many pieces of chicken as can fit without crowding. Fry until golden brown on both sides, 2 to 3 minutes per side. Transfer the chicken to prepared platters. Immediately sprinkle the chicken lightly with salt and squeeze over a generous amount of lemon juice from a halved lemon. Repeat until all of the chicken is cooked, adding more oil to the pan if necessary. Serve.

PANKO

Every Texan cook worth her salt knows breading and frying as well as the back of her hand. My mother, aunts, sisters, and I are no exception. I grew up on breaded and fried chicken, fish, and vegetables: The philosophy was that if it could be eaten, it should be breaded and fried. For years I understood that the texture of the breading was the most important part of this equation. But more often than not, ordinary bread crumbs turned out coatings that were either so heavy that they interfered with the taste of what was inside or too bland to make the deep-frying worth the effort. Then one night several years ago, one of the many cooking shows I love to watch featured panko. I ran out the next day to get some, and my breading was reborn. These flaky bread crumbs from Japan are everything I wanted bread crumbs to be: They provide a thin, crunchy coating and muted but not dull flavor.

chicken with caramelized shallots and shiitake-wine sauce

This is a perfect autumn dish, full of rich flavor and deep color. Be sure to really press down on the chicken when you add it to the pan to help the shallots and green onions stick to the skin and form a sort of caramelized onion crust. I prefer dark meat because it is generally juicier and more flavorful, but this method works very well with both dark and light meat.

MAKES 4 TO 6 SERVINGS

6 bone-in chicken thighs or 4 bone-in or boneless breasts, with skin

Kosher salt and ground black pepper to taste

2 teaspoons olive oil

2 large shallots (about 4 ounces), thinly sliced

2 green onions (white and light green parts), chopped

Ingredients for Shiitake-Wine Sauce (page 167, see Note)

NOTE
The best time to prepare the sauce is indicated in the recipe.

1. Preheat the oven to 350°F.

2. Lightly season the chicken with salt and pepper. In a large, ovenproof skillet, heat the oil over medium heat until hot but not smoking. Add the shallots and green onions and cook, stirring, just until beginning to brown, about 2 minutes. Arrange the chicken over the onions skin-side down and use a spatula to firmly press each piece of chicken into the onions. Cover the skillet and cook until the shallots and green onions are browned and sticking to the skin of the chicken and the chicken is almost completely cooked, 8 to 10 minutes. Uncover and transfer the pan to the oven until the chicken is completely cooked, about 15 minutes.

3. Meanwhile, prepare the shiitake-wine sauce.

4. Transfer the chicken and the caramelized onions to individual plates or a serving platter. Pour over some of the sauce; transfer the remainder to a gravy boat and pass at the table. Serve.

hungarian paprika chicken

My fabulous hairdresser on the set of *Desperate Housewives*, Gabor, shared this recipe with me. In fact, he shared the very recipe his grandmother had used for decades—the card it was on must have been about eighty years old and was written in Hungarian! It took Gabor some time to decipher it, but I'm grateful for his efforts. It's so delicious! It's funny to think that almost every culture has some variation on the big pot of fragrant, nourishing stew. I'm glad to have been introduced to this one.

The bell peppers add sweetness and color; the dish is really beautiful when made with green, red, yellow, and orange peppers, but feel free to use whatever you prefer or can get your hands on. The stew is amazing served over buttered egg noodles. And don't worry about leftovers; this is even better after sitting in the fridge for a day or two.

MAKES 8 TO 10 SERVINGS

- 2 tablespoons olive oil
- 2 yellow onions, chopped
- 3 pounds boneless, skinless chicken thighs, cut into bite-size cubes
- 3 tablespoons sweet paprika
- 1 teaspoon kosher salt
- ¼ teaspoon ground black pepper or to taste
- 4 bell peppers, preferably 1 each, green, red, yellow, and orange, cored and chopped
- 3 tomatoes, chopped
- 1 pound egg noodles
- 1 to 2 tablespoons unsalted butter
- 16 ounces sour cream
- ¼ cup all-purpose flour, or as needed

1. In a Dutch oven or other large pot, heat the oil over medium heat. Add the onions and cook, stirring, until softened and translucent, 6 to 8 minutes. Increase the heat to medium-high and add the chicken. Cook until slightly browned, 8 to 10 minutes.

2. Add the paprika, salt, and pepper and stir to coat the meat. Stir in the peppers and tomatoes. Bring to a simmer. Cover and simmer until the chicken is tender, stirring occasionally, about 20 minutes; the vegetables and chicken will have exuded their liquid to create a fragrant, bubbling stew.

3. Meanwhile, bring a large pot of salted water to a boil. Add the egg noodles and cook according to package directions. Drain thoroughly, return to the pot or a bowl, and toss with the butter. Put aside and keep warm.

4. In a medium bowl, whisk together the sour cream and flour until smooth (for a thicker stew, add more flour). Stir this mixture into the simmering stew, one large spoonful at a time. Bring it all just to a boil and simmer for 5 minutes.

5. Serve hot over the buttered egg noodles.

chalupas

When I was a kid, chalupas were to us what PB&J is to other families. Whenever we were looking for a snack or needed a quick meal, the makings for chalupas were the first things to come out of the fridge. In fact, chalupas were the first thing my mom taught me how to cook. I know now that this is because it was all about *assembling* more than actual *cooking.* And they're fun! Serve them family-style so that each person gets his or her own fried tortilla and can pile on beans, chicken, and any other toppings as high as desired. The effect is beautiful and dramatic.

MAKES 4 TO 8 SERVINGS

- ½ cup vegetable oil or as needed
- 8 corn tortillas
- 4 cups shredded lettuce
- 1½ cups grated or crumbled queso fresco or Cheddar cheese (about 6 ounces)
- ¾ cup sour cream
- 1 large tomato, diced
- 2 avocados, pitted, peeled, and diced
- 2 cups Refried Beans (page 130) or store-bought, warmed
- 2 cups cooked, shredded chicken (page 89), warmed

1. Line a large plate or baking sheet with paper towels. In a large skillet, heat the oil until shimmery and hot but not smoking. Fry the tortillas one at a time until firm but not burned, about 1 minute per side. Transfer to the paper towels and let cool for 5 minutes.

2. Place the lettuce, cheese, sour cream, tomato, and avocado in separate serving bowls.

3. Spread the refried beans on each of the tortillas. Sprinkle the shredded chicken on top of the beans. Arrange the chalupas on a platter and serve them with the serving bowls of toppings so everyone can build their own!

chicken salad sandwiches

I remember often seeing mountains of these little finger sandwiches in my Aunt Elsa's kitchen (see photograph on page 76). She would make vast numbers and freeze them in advance of big catered events like baby showers or wedding receptions (see below for tips on getting ahead). I love these creamy and crunchy chicken salad sandwiches—with lots of mayonnaise, crunchy celery and nuts, and sweet grapes and relish, they are perfect picnic fare. Judging by how quickly I've seen them fly off the serving platter, my friends and family agree! Red onions are a little sweeter than white ones; use what you like.

MAKES ABOUT 4 CUPS CHICKEN SALAD; 8 SERVINGS

- 3 cups cooked, chopped chicken (page 89) or turkey
- 1 cup halved green and red grapes
- ½ cup chopped pecans or walnuts
- ¼ cup chopped celery
- ¼ cup chopped white or red onion
- ¼ cup sweet pickle relish
- ¼ teaspoon kosher salt
- ¼ teaspoon ground black pepper
- 1 cup mayonnaise
- 16 slices white sandwich bread
- 4 tablespoons (½ stick) unsalted butter, softened (optional)

1. In a medium mixing bowl, place the chicken, grapes, nuts, celery, onion, relish, salt, and pepper. Stir until well combined. Add the mayonnaise and stir until the chicken is well coated.

2. Arrange a few slices of bread in a neat stack and use a serrated knife to slice off the crusts. Repeat until all of the bread slices are trimmed.

3. Place about a ½ cup chicken salad on half of the slices. Place the remaining slices on top. Slice each sandwich into 4 squares or triangles. Arrange on a platter and serve.

FROM AUNT ELSA'S KITCHEN

Aunt Elsa would make these ahead of time for a party and refrigerate them for a few hours or freeze them for up to a week and remove them from the freezer the morning of the event. Her secret was to spread a thin coat of butter on the bread, which prevents the sandwiches from getting soggy without changing any flavor.

To make ahead, spread a light coat of butter on one side of each slice of bread. After slicing as directed above, cover the sandwiches with wax paper, and then cover with a damp towel. Refrigerate until needed.

For longer storage, cover the platter of sandwiches with plastic wrap and freeze. Uncover the sandwiches and let stand at room temperature for a few hours before serving.

ROASTED AND POACHED CHICKEN

Many recipes in this chapter and beyond the pages of this book call for cooked chicken. Here are my two favorite ways to cook chicken when it's going to be used in a prepared dish.

Roasted Boneless, Skinless Breasts

MAKES ABOUT 4 CUPS SHREDDED OR CHOPPED MEAT

2 boneless, skinless chicken breasts (¾ to 1 pound)

2 teaspoons olive oil

Kosher salt and ground black pepper

Preheat the oven to 375°F. Lightly coat with cooking spray a small cast-iron pan or other baking dish. Place the chicken breasts in the pan and rub the tops with oil. Sprinkle with salt and pepper. Cook until the juices run clear when pricked with a knife, 20 to 25 minutes. Set aside to cool. When cool enough to handle, shred or cut as directed in the recipe.

Poached Chicken

BREASTS MAKE ABOUT 8 CUPS SHREDDED OR CHOPPED MEAT
WHOLE CHICKEN MAKES ABOUT 6 CUPS SHREDDED OR CHOPPED MEAT

2 1½-pound whole bone-in chicken breasts (4 individual breasts)
    or 1 4-pound whole chicken

1 large onion, quartered

1 clove garlic, smashed with the side of a knife

1 whole serrano pepper

In a large saucepan or Dutch oven, place the chicken, onion, garlic, and serrano. Add cold water to cover and bring to a boil over high heat. Reduce the heat and simmer until the chicken is opaque and the juices run clear when the thickest part of the meat is pricked with a knife, 15 to 20 minutes for breasts, about 30 minutes for whole chicken. Transfer the chicken to a plate to cool; reserve the broth for another use. When the chicken is cool enough to handle, remove and discard the skin and bones; chop or use your hands to shred the meat as directed in the recipe.

bbq chicken pizza

This festive pizza comes from my sister Esmeralda. I often make several and put them out at Super Bowl parties. It makes a family-friendly weeknight dinner with a salad.

MAKES 4 TO
6 SERVINGS

2 packages refrigerated pizza crust dough

All-purpose flour, for rolling the dough

Cornmeal, for dusting

BBQ Sauce (page 164)

2 boneless, skinless chicken breasts (¾ to 1 pound), cooked and cut into bite-size pieces (page 89)

1 small red onion, sliced (optional)

1 can pitted black olives, drained and chopped (optional)

1 8-ounce package shredded Colby cheese (about 2 cups)

1 8-ounce package shredded Monterey Jack cheese (about 2 cups)

1 cup (4 ounces) grated Parmesan cheese (optional)

1. Position the oven rack or racks in the lower third of the oven and preheat the oven to 425°F.

2. Let the dough stand at room temperature for 20 minutes. On a lightly floured surface, roll each pizza dough into a round. Lightly dust 2 large, round pizza stones or baking sheets with cornmeal. Around the edge of the pizza, make a little raised crust about ½ inch wide.

3. Divide the BBQ sauce between the dough rounds and spread to within ½ inch of the edge.

4. In a medium bowl, place the cut chicken, onion, olives, and ¾ cup each of the Colby and Monterey Jack cheeses (1½ cups total). Spread the chicken mixture over the sauce on each dough round.

5. Scatter the remaining cheese over each pizza. If desired, sprinkle Parmesan over each as well.

6. Bake the two pizzas until the cheese is melted and the crust is golden brown, 18 to 22 minutes. Let stand 10 minutes before slicing and serving.

flautas

A giant platter of flautas is a stunning sight on a table, and the contrasting flavors and textures make it a fabulous eating experience as well. Chicken is rolled in corn tortillas and fried until crispy. The flautas are arranged on a platter, topped with a beautiful, pale green sauce that is at once silky and tart, drizzled with luscious Mexican sour cream, and sprinkled with creamy queso fresco. The result is a crunchy, creamy, and chewy burst of divine flavor.

Mexican sour cream or crema is the Mexican version of crème fraîche, and both are milder versions of American sour cream. You can find crema in the refrigerated section of grocery stories that carry Latin ingredients. Crème fraîche is thicker, so if you use it instead, stir it well to loosen the consistency before drizzling.

MAKES 8 TO 10 SERVINGS

1 28-ounce can cooked tomatillos, drained

1 ripe avocado, pitted and peeled

Kosher salt to taste

About 50 corn tortillas

2 whole (4 individual) bone-in chicken breasts (about 3 pounds total), cooked and shredded (page 89)

2 cups vegetable oil or as needed, for frying

½ cup Mexican sour cream (crema Mexicana) or crème fraîche, for serving

1½ cups grated or crumbled queso fresco (about 6 ounces), for serving

Special equipment: 50 wooden toothpicks

1. In a blender, place the drained tomatillos and avocado. Blend until very well pureed. Add salt to taste and set aside.

2. Wrap about 10 tortillas in a clean kitchen towel and heat for 2 minutes in the microwave; this will make them soft for rolling into flautas. Spread about 2 tablespoons of the chicken in a straight line just below the center of the tortilla. Starting at the side closest to you, roll the tortilla into a tight cylinder and secure with a toothpick. Repeat with the remaining tortillas and chicken.

3. Line a baking sheet or platter with paper towels. In a large skillet, pour the oil to about ½ inch and heat to about 365°F. over medium heat. Place several flautas in the oil and fry until golden brown on the bottom, 2 to 3 minutes. Turn over and fry until golden brown, 2 to 3 minutes. Use tongs to remove the flautas from the oil, making sure to turn them straight up to let the oil run out of the cylinder. Transfer to the paper towel–lined pan to drain. Continue until all the flautas are fried. Remove and discard the toothpicks.

4. Arrange the fried flautas on a serving platter. Pour over some of the reserved green sauce; transfer the rest to a gravy boat to pass at the table. Drizzle with the sour cream (if using crème fraîche, stir it first if it's very stiff) and sprinkle over queso fresco. Serve.

enchiladas rojas (red enchiladas)

When I was growing up, enchiladas were a family affair. On enchilada night, my sisters and I knew we would be called upon to take our positions alongside our mom in the kitchen: one sister fried the tortillas, another dipped them in the sauce, another (usually me) stuffed them, and the last rolled and transferred them to the pan. I can never think about enchiladas without remembering all those happy times in the kitchen.

Not everyone in the house loved onions as much as my dad did, so Mom had us add the onions to only half of the enchiladas. She'd stick a toothpick in the pan with the onions to mark it, and everyone could sit down to enjoy the same meal.

MAKES 8 SERVINGS

- 10 medium tomatoes, quartered
- 10 dried ancho chiles
- 8 garlic cloves
- 1 cup broth from cooked chicken, or store-bought
- 1¼ cups vegetable oil or as needed
- Kosher salt to taste
- About 48 corn tortillas
- 1 4-pound whole chicken, poached and shredded (page 89)
- 1 yellow onion, finely chopped (optional)
- 3 cups grated or crumbled queso fresco (about 12 ounces) or shredded Mexican Cheese
- Mexican Rice (page 124), for serving
- Refried Beans (page 130), for serving

1. For the sauce: Place the tomatoes and chiles in a large saucepan and cover with cold water. Bring to a boil and cook gently until the chiles are tender, about 10 minutes. Drain and remove the stems from the chiles. Working in batches if necessary, place the tomatoes, chiles, garlic, and chicken broth in the work bowl of a food processor. Process until well pureed.

2. In a large skillet, heat ¼ cup of the oil over medium heat until shimmery and hot but not smoking. Add the sauce and bring to a simmer. Simmer for 10 minutes. Remove the sauce from the heat. Set aside until cool.

3. For the enchiladas: Line a baking sheet or platter with paper towels. In a small skillet, heat 1 cup of oil until shimmery and hot but not smoking. Lightly fry the tortillas one at a time just until softened, 5 to 10 seconds per side. Transfer to the paper towel–lined pan to drain.

4. Preheat the oven to 350°F. Lightly coat one or two baking dishes with cooking spray.

(recipe continues)

5. Working with one tortilla at a time, dip a tortilla in the red sauce, lightly soaking both sides completely. Place the tortilla in a baking dish and arrange about 1 tablespoon of chicken in a line just above the center of the tortilla. Sprinkle over a bit of onion, if desired. Tightly roll up the tortilla and place it at one end of the baking dish. Repeat with all of the tortillas until all the enchiladas are snug in the dish. Use a second baking dish if necessary.

6. When all of the enchiladas are rolled and snug in a baking dish, pour over any remaining sauce. Sprinkle the cheese over the top and cover the pan(s) with foil. Place the baking dishes in the oven until the cheese is melted and the enchiladas are heated through, 15 to 20 minutes. Remove from the oven. Serve directly from the dish, using a spatula to scoop out the enchiladas. Serve with Mexican rice and refried beans.

DRIED CHILES

My favorite dried chiles, also called peppers, are ancho, pasilla, and chipotle (dried and in adobo). Anchos are dried poblano peppers. They are large and very dark and have a sweet flavor. They are sometimes mistakenly labeled "pasilla" or "ancho pasilla," but it's easy to tell the difference; while true anchos are squat and wide, true pasillas are very long and thin.

Pasilla chiles, also called negro chiles, have a mellow flavor. Both ancho and pasilla are very widely used in Mexican cooking, especially in moles and soups. I use both in my fantastic Tortilla Soup (page 45), which owes much of its depth to the dried chile.

Chipotle chiles are dried, smoked jalapeños and are sold both dried and in cans mixed with a highly seasoned tomato sauce. They add smoky flavor and heat to Chili con Carne (page 110) and Chipotle Aïoli (page 162).

turkey shepherd's pie

A dear friend from London gave me this recipe and a bit of good English advice: The key to great shepherd's pie is the ketchup. So taste the turkey mixture before adding it to the baking dish and add another spoonful or two of ketchup if desired. The chili powder gives good flavor but no heat, so don't let it scare you.

MAKES 8 SERVINGS

Vegetable oil or cooking spray, for the baking dish

2 pounds russet potatoes, peeled and cut into small cubes

Kosher salt

½ cup buttermilk

Ground black pepper

2 pounds ground turkey or beef

1 large yellow onion, finely chopped

2 medium carrots, cut into ½-inch pieces

2 celery ribs, cut into ½-inch pieces

1 garlic clove, minced

1 14½-ounce can whole tomatoes with juice, chopped

¼ cup ketchup

1 tablespoon chili powder

½ cup grated Cheddar cheese (about 2 ounces)

1. Preheat the oven to 350°F. Lightly brush or spray a 9 × 13-inch baking dish with vegetable oil. Set aside.

2. Place the potatoes in a large saucepan with enough lightly salted water to cover by 1 inch. Bring to a boil over medium-high heat and simmer until the potatoes are tender when pierced with a sharp knife, about 15 minutes. Drain and return the potatoes to the saucepan. Add the buttermilk and use a potato masher to mash the potatoes until smooth. Add salt and pepper to taste. Set aside.

3. Meanwhile, in a large, nonstick skillet, cook the turkey or beef over medium heat, breaking up the meat with a spoon, until it loses its pink color, about 7 minutes. Stir in the onion, carrots, celery, and garlic and cook, stirring occasionally, until the vegetables have softened, about 5 minutes. Stir in the tomatoes, ketchup, and chili powder and bring to a simmer. Season to taste with salt and pepper.

4. Spoon the turkey mixture into the prepared baking dish. Spread the mashed potatoes over the turkey and sprinkle with the cheese. Bake until the juices are bubbling and the cheese is melted, 30 to 40 minutes. Let stand 5 to 10 minutes before serving.

beef main courses

Texas is beef country. Although we weren't cattle ranchers, we had cows—I think it must be one of the unwritten laws of Texas that if you have a ranch, you have cattle. By the time I was ten I knew every cut of meat and how to best cook each to bring out its natural goodness. I learned that flank and skirt are among the most flavorful (and cheapest!) cuts of meat, and that cooking bone-in roasts gives meatier flavor than boneless. I especially learned to pay attention to the goal when choosing a cut and how to cook it; to use fatty skirt or flank when the meat is destined for tacos or fajitas and meltingly tender filet mignon when I'm serving an elegant sauce.

Living on the ranch surrounded by live animals taught me something else: All our food deserves respect. To this end, I buy only grass-fed beef even though it is more expensive. Cows cannot properly digest grain; it is not their natural diet. I would rather eat beef that has been raised in a way that respects its natural state. If you don't have a grocery store that carries grass-fed meat near you, check out eatwild.com, which will help you find local farms with pasture-fed meat.

beer-braised brisket

chili-rubbed skirt steak tacos

flank steak with lime marinade

chicken fried steak with white gravy

aunt didi's carne guisada

filets mignons with sweet balsamic reduction

chili con carne

beef bolognese

crock-pot cuban ropa vieja

meat loaf

stuffed green peppers

mexican lasagna

beer-braised brisket

Brisket is a cornerstone of Texas cooking, as much a part of the culinary fabric as sweet iced tea and biscuits. This version is a great "prep it and forget it" dish. You can pull it together and toss it all in the roasting pan in just a few minutes, and then put it in the oven and do something else for 3 hours. The house smells amazing while it's cooking and the result is meltingly tender brisket and a tangy-sweet sauce. Toward the end of cooking, toss a green salad and make some White Rice (page 126)—or if you're feeling more ambitious, place the Broccoli and Rice Casserole (page 123) in the oven 30 minutes before the brisket is done—and dinner is served!

MAKES 8 TO 10 SERVINGS

1 4- to 5-pound beef brisket

1 large yellow onion, sliced

1 12-ounce bottle chili sauce (about 1 generous cup)

2 tablespoons brown sugar

5 garlic cloves, minced

1 12-ounce can beer (not dark)

1 tablespoon cornstarch (optional)

1. Preheat the oven to 350°F.

2. In a large roasting pan (with a lid, if possible), place the brisket fat-side up. Spread the onion on top. In a medium mixing bowl, place the chili sauce, brown sugar, garlic, and beer. Stir until well blended. Pour the sauce on top of the meat. Tightly cover the pan with the lid or aluminum foil.

3. Bake for 3 hours. If you'd like to thicken the gravy, transfer the brisket to a platter and keep warm. Place the cornstarch in a small dish and add 2 tablespoons water. Stir until dissolved and stir into the cooking liquid. Bring to a boil and cook for 1 minute, stirring constantly.

4. To serve, cut the brisket across the grain into ¼-inch slices. Arrange the slices on a platter and pour some of the sauce over the brisket. Transfer the remaining sauce to a gravy boat to pass at the table.

chili-rubbed skirt steak tacos

At Beso these tacos are served as an appetizer, but some people love them so much that they make a meal of them, ordering VeraCruz Corn (page 151) on the side. Guests often look at the dish's name and exclaim, "I don't like spicy!" but I always assure them that the chili powder adds only beautiful color and nice flavor. I promise it does not *pica,* as my Aunt Elsa would say, meaning that it's not spicy.

**MAKES 4 TO
6 SERVINGS**

2 tablespoons chili powder

2 pounds skirt steak

Kosher salt to taste

12 corn tortillas

1 cup Chunky Guacamole with Serrano Peppers (page 19)

Special equipment:
12 wooden toothpicks

1. Lightly oil the grill grate and prepare a medium-hot grill.

2. Rub the chili powder onto both sides of the steak and sprinkle generously with salt. Grill the steak, turning once, about 5 minutes per side for medium-rare, or longer to taste. Transfer to a cutting board and let stand for 5 minutes.

3. Stack the tortillas on a cutting board and use a sharp, thin-bladed knife to trim them into 4-inch squares. Heat a *comal* (page 173) or flat cast-iron griddle over medium heat. Place 1 to 2 tortilla squares on the *comal,* or as many as will fit without crowding, and heat until warm and soft. Transfer to a plate and cover with a clean kitchen towel to keep warm while you heat the remaining tortilla squares.

4. Place a warm tortilla on a work surface with its points going up and down, like a diamond. Holding the knife at a roughly 45-degree angle to the cutting surface, cut the steak diagonally across the grain into thin strips. Place 2 to 3 strips across the center of the diamond. Top with a generous spoonful of guacamole. Pull the tortilla together corner to corner (so it looks like a triangle) and secure it with a toothpick. Place the taco on a serving platter and repeat with the remaining ingredients. Serve.

flank steak with lime marinade

As its name suggests, flank steak comes from the flank of the beef, between the ribs and the hips. I've been eating and loving flank and skirt steak, which comes from the same area, my whole life, since they are used abundantly in Latin cooking. For some reason, these cuts have yet to reach a wider audience. This is curious to me, for what flank steak lacks in tenderness it more than makes up in fabulous beefy flavor. Cut it across, not with, the grain so it's less chewy. This tangy marinade is great for any cut of beef. As with any marinade, the longer you can let the steak sit in it, the better it'll be.

MAKES 4 SERVINGS

FOR THE MARINADE

- 3 tablespoons extra-virgin olive oil
- 3 tablespoons fresh lime juice (from about 2 limes)
- 4 garlic cloves, thinly sliced
- 1 serrano pepper, cored, seeded if desired, and thinly sliced
- 2 teaspoons chili powder
- 1 teaspoon ground cumin
- ½ teaspoon kosher salt

FOR THE STEAK

- 1½ pounds flank steak

1. In a shallow dish, place the oil, lime juice, garlic, serrano, chili powder, cumin, and salt and stir until well blended. Lay the flank steak in the dish and turn a few times until thoroughly coated. Cover with plastic wrap and place in the refrigerator for at least 2 hours and up to overnight (the longer, the better), turning occasionally.

2. Lightly oil the grill grate and prepare a medium-high grill. Pat the steak dry with paper towels. Grill for about 8 to 10 minutes total, turning once, for medium-rare. Transfer to a cutting board and let stand for 5 minutes. Use a long, thin knife held at a slant to cut the steak across the grain into thin slices. Serve immediately.

FROM AUNT ELSA'S KITCHEN

Be sure to thoroughly dry the steak by patting it with paper towels before you grill it. If the steak is too moist, it'll steam rather than sear, and you won't get a nice crust.

chicken fried steak with white gravy

The trick here is to add a lot of seasoning to the dredging flour and then use the leftover seasoned flour to make the gravy. Serve with Garlic Mashed Potatoes (page 149).

MAKES 8 TO 10 SERVINGS

- 3 pounds beef round roast or thin steaks or pretenderized "cube" steaks
- 4 large eggs
- 1 cup all-purpose flour, plus more if needed
- 1 tablespoon kosher salt (see Note)
- 2 teaspoons ground black pepper (see Note)
- ½ cup vegetable oil, plus more if needed
- 4 cups whole milk

NOTE
Or use 1 tablespoon Season-All in place of the salt and pepper.

1. If using a roast, slice the meat with the grain into ½- to ¾-inch-thick slices. If using round steaks, halve them horizontally to create thinner steaks if necessary. Lay the steaks on a work surface and use a meat mallet to pound them to ¼-inch thickness. If using cubed steak, no slicing or tenderizing is required.

2. Heat a warming drawer or preheat the oven to 175°F.

3. In a wide, shallow bowl, beat the eggs. In a second wide shallow bowl, place the flour, salt, and pepper and whisk until well blended. Coat a steak on both sides with egg, and then dredge in the seasoned flour, coating both sides. Transfer to a baking sheet or platter and repeat with the remaining steaks. Set the remaining flour aside.

4. In a large skillet, heat the oil over medium heat until shimmery and hot but not smoking. Place enough steaks in the hot oil that they fit without crowding; do not pack the skillet or they will take longer. Fry until well browned, 4 to 6 minutes per side (longer if steaks are thick or not well tenderized). Transfer to a serving platter and continue until all the steaks are cooked, adding more oil to the pan if necessary. Keep the transferred steaks warm in a warming drawer or the oven. Do not cover with foil or they will become soggy.

5. Drain the skillet of all but 2 tablespoons oil; leave any bits of coating in the pan. Return the pan to the heat and slowly stir in ⅓ cup of the reserved seasoned flour, scraping the bottom of the pan to loosen the cooked-on bits. When the drippings and the flour are well mixed, stir in the milk. Simmer the gravy until thickened, 10 to 15 minutes.

6. Drizzle some gravy over the steaks and serve; pass any remaining gravy at the table.

aunt didi's carne guisada

This classic Tex-Mex stew (see photograph on page 10) is rich and delicious without the hours of simmering that most stews require. I cannot imagine ever eating this without Aunt Edna's Homemade Flour Tortillas (page 171) to soak up every last drop of flavorful sauce.

MAKES 4 SERVINGS

1 tablespoon olive oil

2 pounds beef sirloin, cut into 1-inch cubes

1 medium white onion, sliced

4 garlic cloves, minced

½ green bell pepper, sliced

2 tablespoons ground cumin

1 teaspoon kosher salt

1 teaspoon ground black pepper

1 8-ounce can tomato sauce

Mexican Rice (page 124), for serving

Refried Beans (page 130), for serving

Aunt Edna's Homemade Flour Tortillas (page 171), warm for serving

1. In a large skillet, heat the oil over medium heat. Add the meat and cook, stirring occasionally, until the meat is browned in spots but still a little red in the middle, about 5 minutes.

2. Add the onion, garlic, and bell pepper and stir to combine. Add the cumin, salt, and pepper and stir to combine. Stir in the tomato sauce and 1 cup of water. Bring to a boil. Reduce the heat to low and simmer for 5 minutes. Serve with Mexican rice, refried beans, and warm tortillas.

FROM AUNT ELSA'S KITCHEN
For a thicker gravy, after cooking use a slotted spoon to transfer the meat and vegetables to a serving bowl. Combine 1 tablespoon all-purpose flour with ¼ cup water and stir until smooth. Whisk this slurry into the gravy and simmer for 1 to 2 minutes until thickened. Pour the gravy over the meat and serve.

filets mignons with sweet balsamic reduction

The most important thing about preparing filets mignons is to use a light hand with the steaks themselves. To bring out their melting tenderness, absolutely all they need is a little salt and pepper and to be sautéed in some butter or olive oil. Here, they are drizzled with an elegant reduced balsamic sauce with deep, almost molasses flavor and a welcome bite at the finish. Try this dish with Brazilian Leeks (page 142). The filets are also wonderful with the heartier Shiitake-Wine Sauce (page 167).

MAKES 4 SERVINGS

4 4- to 6-ounce filet mignon steaks

Kosher salt and ground black pepper

1 tablespoon unsalted butter

Sweet Balsamic Reduction (page 165)

1. Season both sides of the filets with salt and pepper. In a large skillet, melt the butter over medium heat. Add the steaks and cook 4 to 5 minutes per side for medium-rare.

2. Arrange the filets on 4 individual plates or on a serving platter. Drizzle the sauce over each filet and serve.

FROM AUNT ELSA'S KITCHEN
Red meat tastes best when cooked to medium-rare, which means the interior of the meat is warm and very red and juicy.

chili con carne

These days I'm more likely to eat Chili con Carne with flavorful Corn Bread (page 181), but when I was a kid, "Frito pie" was one of our favorite after-school snacks: Place a generous handful of Fritos or other corn chips in the bottom of a bowl, ladle over some hot Chili con Carne, and top with cheddar cheese. Every delicious bite is cheesy, crunchy, and meaty!

Mexican chorizo is a fresh (not dried) pork sausage seasoned with chiles; it makes all the difference between this Chili con Carne and more basic versions.

This chili is better if it's made a day ahead.

MAKES 12 SERVINGS

- 8 dried chipotle chiles (see page 96)
- 2 28-ounce cans whole tomatoes with juice
- Kosher salt
- 12 ounces Mexican chorizo, casing removed
- 1 medium white onion, chopped
- 4 pounds ground beef or turkey
- 3 15-ounce cans low-sodium whole pinto beans or 4 cups drained Borracho Beans (page 128)
- Corn Bread (page 181), for serving
- Grated cheddar cheese, for serving

1. In a medium saucepan, bring 3 cups of water to a boil. Add the chiles and boil gently until soft, about 10 minutes. Drain and set aside to cool. When cool enough to handle, remove the stems and seeds, if desired, from the chiles. (Note: *Leaving the seeds will make your chili con carne spicier!*) Rinse them well and place in a large mixing bowl. Add the tomatoes and their juice and stir until combined.

2. Working in batches, transfer the tomato-chipotle mixture to a blender and puree until smooth. Add salt to taste and set aside.

3. In a large stew pot over medium heat, cook the chorizo and onion, stirring occasionally and breaking up the chorizo with a spoon, until the chorizo is lightly browned and the onions softened, 10 to 15 minutes. Add the ground beef or turkey and cook, stirring occasionally, until the meat is browned. Stir in the tomato-chipotle puree and the beans. Heat until hot and add salt to taste. Serve with corn bread and cheese.

beef bolognese

I ran track in high school, and one day my coach told me to eat more pasta to increase my energy. So I went straight home and told my mom that I needed her to pick up a bunch of spaghetti sauce at the store. My mother pointed out that the jars were too expensive—about $2 a jar back then, generally a lot more nowadays—for the amount I was likely to eat (I could eat pasta morning, noon, and night). She wisely suggested I pick up a case of tomato sauce (6 cans for $1!) and get to work. Believe me, a lot of trial and error happened between my first pot and the recipe you see here. It took years to get the right mix of spices. But to this day, I would always rather start a pot with a can of tomato sauce than open any jar of store-bought spaghetti sauce. This bolognese stores beautifully for several months in the freezer, so sometimes I just mix up a batch to store and pull out in a pinch!

MAKES ABOUT 10 CUPS; 8 TO 10 SERVINGS

1½ cups chopped yellow onions

8 cloves garlic, minced

½ cup chopped celery

½ cup chopped carrots

½ cup olive oil

Kosher salt and ground black pepper

2 pounds ground beef or turkey

1½ cups Beef Broth (page 114) or store-bought low-sodium beef broth, plus more if needed

½ cup dry red wine

½ cup dry white wine

4 cups tomato sauce, plus more if needed

¼ cup ketchup

2 fresh or dried bay leaves

2 sprigs of fresh thyme

3 tablespoons dried oregano

1. In the work bowl of a food processor, pulse the onions, garlic, celery, and carrots until finely chopped.

2. In a Dutch oven or other large stockpot, heat the oil over medium heat. Add the onion mixture with a pinch each of salt and pepper and cook, stirring occasionally, until softened, about 5 minutes.

3. Add the ground beef and cook, stirring occasionally, until cooked through, 8 to 10 minutes. Add the broth and the red and white wines and simmer for 10 minutes.

4. Add the tomato sauce, ketchup, bay leaves, thyme, oregano, 1 teaspoon salt, and ½ teaspoon pepper. Bring to a boil. Reduce the heat to low and simmer, covered, for 30 minutes. Check occasionally during cooking and add more broth or tomato sauce if a saucier consistency is desired.

5. Remove and discard the bay leaves and thyme sprigs. Serve the beef bolognese over any pasta.

crock-pot cuban ropa vieja

MAKES 8 TO 10 SERVINGS

2½ pounds beef flank steak

6 tablespoons ground cumin

4 tablespoons olive oil or as needed

2 cups Beef Broth (recipe follows) or store-bought low-sodium beef broth

2 8-ounce cans tomato sauce

2 6-ounce cans tomato paste

2 tablespoons distilled vinegar

8 garlic cloves, minced

1½ teaspoons kosher salt

1 large yellow or white onion, chopped

1 green bell pepper, cored, seeded, and sliced into ½-inch strips

1 red bell pepper, cored, seeded, and sliced into ½-inch strips

1 bunch of fresh cilantro, leaves chopped

White Rice (page 126), for serving

Black Beans (page 127), for serving

Fried Plantains (page 153), for serving

Ropa vieja translates literally to "old clothes," which is what the shredded meat, visually, may bring to mind. The smell and taste of this dish, however, are nothing short of heavenly. Please don't be intimidated by the long list of ingredients. There is only a little bit of chopping required; the whole point is to put a bunch of things together and forget about it for hours (although you're welcome to taste along the way if you prefer—or can't resist!). The shredded meat should stand for at least 15 minutes before serving, but if you have more time, let it stand longer, as it just gets better and better.

This dish's origins are Caribbean, so serve it with other foods from the same region, especially white rice, black beans, and plantains.

1. Rub the steak on both sides with 3 tablespoons of the cumin. In a large skillet, heat 2 tablespoons of oil over medium-high heat until shimmery and hot but not smoking. Add the flank steak and cook until browned on both sides, about 5 minutes per side. Transfer to a large Crock-Pot.

2. In a large mixing bowl, mix together the broth, tomato sauce, tomato paste, vinegar, garlic, salt, the remaining 3 tablespoons of cumin, and the remaining 2 tablespoons of olive oil. Stir until well blended. Add the onion, bell peppers, and cilantro. Stir until well blended. Pour the tomato mixture over the meat in the Crock-Pot.

3. Cover and cook on high for 4 hours, or on low for up to 10 hours. The meat is ready when it falls apart when pierced with a fork. Remove the meat from the sauce and use two forks to pull apart the meat, shredding it into strings. Return the shredded meat to the sauce and let stand for 15 minutes. Serve the shredded meat with the flavorful juices spooned over and with white rice, black beans, and fried plantains on the side.

(recipe continues)

beef broth

Making broth at home is so easy, and there's not all that sodium and other who-knows-what-else in broth you make yourself.

MAKES ABOUT 3 QUARTS

- 3 pounds beef bones or a combination of bones, oxtails, and short ribs
- 1 large onion, coarsely chopped
- 2 medium leeks (white and light green parts only), coarsely chopped
- 2 medium carrots, coarsely chopped
- 1 celery rib with leaves, coarsely chopped
- 1½ teaspoons tomato paste
- 4 sprigs of fresh thyme or ½ teaspoon dried thyme
- 4 sprigs of fresh parsley
- ¼ teaspoon whole black peppercorns
- 1 fresh or dried bay leaf

1. Preheat the oven to 450°F.

2. Spread the bones in a flameproof roasting pan. Bake until the bones are brown, 30 to 45 minutes.

3. Transfer the bones to a stockpot. Pour the fat out of the pan. Place the roasting pan over high heat. Pour 2 cups of water into the pan and bring to a boil, scraping up the browned bits in the pan with a wooden spoon. Pour this liquid into the stockpot. Add the onion, leeks, carrots, and celery.

4. Add cold water to cover the bones by 2 inches. Bring to a boil over high heat. Use a large spoon to skim off any foam that rises to the surface. Add the tomato paste, thyme, parsley, peppercorns, and bay leaf. Reduce the heat to low and simmer, partially covered, until the broth is full flavored, at least 2 hours and up to 8 hours. Strain the broth through a mesh strainer and discard the solids. Let cool. If desired, refrigerate the stock and remove and discard the solidified fat from the surface.

5. Store in tightly covered containers in the refrigerator for up to 5 days or freeze up to 6 months.

meat loaf

I grew up fully immersed in the rich culinary culture and history of Mexico and Texas. It took many years for me to realize that there was literally a whole world of food and culture beyond what I knew so well. When it began to dawn on me, I set out to discover what a meal without tortillas, cheese, and Mexican rice would look like. I longed to begin my new education with the most "American" thing I could think of. And, I ask you, what is more American than meat loaf? This is the first recipe that opened my eyes to cooking meat in a completely different way. It's the same meat loaf I make to this day.

MAKES 4 TO 6 SERVINGS

1½ pounds lean ground beef

¾ cup uncooked oatmeal

¾ cup milk

1 large egg, lightly beaten

¼ cup chopped yellow or white onion

2 garlic cloves, minced

1 teaspoon kosher salt

½ teaspoon ground black pepper

½ cup ketchup

2 tablespoons packed light or dark brown sugar

2 tablespoons Worcestershire sauce

1 tablespoon mustard

1. Preheat the oven to 350°F. In a large bowl, place the ground beef, oatmeal, milk, egg, onion, garlic, salt, and pepper. Use your hands to mix until well blended.

2. Pack the mixture into a 9 × 5-inch loaf pan and set aside.

3. In a glass measuring cup or small bowl, place the ketchup, brown sugar, Worcestershire sauce, and mustard. Stir until completely blended.

4. Pour the sauce over the meat loaf. Bake until cooked and bubbling slightly around the edges, about 1 hour. Let stand 5 minutes.

5. If desired, use a spatula to remove the meat loaf from the pan. Cut crosswise and serve.

stuffed green peppers

Sweet bell peppers are stuffed with a very tasty beef filling and topped with queso fresco and pico de gallo, forming the green, white, red pattern that I love so much! This is a tasty and quick-to-make weeknight meal, which is also pretty enough to serve to company.

MAKES 4 SERVINGS

Cooking spray for the baking dish

4 large green bell peppers

½ pound ground beef

2 tablespoons chopped onion

1 8-ounce can tomato sauce

1 cup dried bread crumbs

1 teaspoon kosher salt

½ teaspoon ground black pepper

½ to 1 cup grated or crumbled queso fresco (about 2 to 4 ounces), for serving (see page 152)

Pico de Gallo (page 20), for serving

1. Preheat the oven to 350°F. Bring a medium saucepan of water to a boil. Coat a small baking dish with cooking spray.

2. Cut a thin slice from the stem end of each green pepper. Pull out the core, remove the seeds, and rinse the peppers inside and out. Add the peppers to the boiling water and simmer for 5 minutes. Drain well and set aside.

3. Meanwhile, in a medium skillet over medium heat, add the beef and onion. Cook, stirring and breaking up the meat with a spoon, until mostly browned with some pink left, about 5 minutes. Stir in the tomato sauce, bread crumbs, salt, and pepper.

4. Stuff the peppers lightly with the meat mixture and put the tops on. Stand them upright in the baking dish. Cover the dish with aluminum foil and bake for 35 minutes. Remove the foil and bake 15 minutes longer.

5. To serve, sprinkle each stuffed pepper with queso fresco and top with a spoonful of pico de gallo.

mexican lasagna

This is a really fun dish to make and serve. It's great for parties or to bring to potlucks and it's convenient. You can assemble it completely and then freeze it (let it stand at room temperature for 1 hour before baking as directed below).

I like to make it in two round cake pans because it looks really pretty when you slice it. Use any saucy salsa that you like; don't use pico de gallo, which is too chunky.

Shredded Mexican cheese is a packaged combination of three to four cheeses, usually Cheddar, Monterey Jack, queso quesadilla, and asadero. It adds more complex flavor than a single cheese and melts really well. Of course, you can grate your own selection of cheeses, but I like the convenience of the preshredded and packaged version.

MAKES 6 TO 8 SERVINGS

Cooking spray for the cake pans and foil

2 pounds ground beef or turkey

Kosher salt and ground black pepper

½ cup Chicken Broth (page 51) or store-bought low-sodium chicken broth

10 flour tortillas

1 16-ounce jar Pace Picante Sauce or other store-bought or homemade saucy salsa

1 16-ounce package shredded Mexican cheese

1 8-ounce container sour cream

2 4.5-ounce cans chopped green chiles

1. Preheat the oven to 375°F. Coat two 8-inch cake pans with cooking spray.

2. In a large skillet over medium heat, cook the beef, stirring and breaking it up with a spoon, until browned. Season with salt and pepper. Set aside.

3. Pour the chicken broth in a large shallow dish and add the tortillas. Soak about 5 minutes; you want them soft but not mushy. Set aside ½ cup salsa and 1 cup cheese.

4. Place 1 tortilla on the bottom of each cake pan. In each pan, layer as follows: spread about 2 tablespoons of sour cream on top of the tortilla. Sprinkle about 2 tablespoons chiles over the sour cream, followed by about ½ cup of the browned meat, 2 tablespoons salsa, and ⅓ cup shredded cheese. Top with a tortilla. Repeat to make 3 more layers of filling. Finish with a tortilla on top. (You'll have a stack of 5 tortillas and 4 layers of filling.) Divide the reserved salsa and cheese between the two pans, spreading the salsa to cover the tortilla and sprinkling the cheese to cover the salsa.

5. Spray one side of 2 sheets of aluminum foil with cooking spray and place them oiled-side down over the pans. Bake for 30 minutes, until hot and bubbling around the edges. Serve hot.

delectable sides

Perhaps because of the seemingly endless abundance of fresh food my aunts and mother produced when I was a child, I love the sight of a table full of many dishes and different flavors. I think the bounty of this chapter reflects that. Yes, these are my favorite side dishes, but many can easily be served as the main course, and a collection of any of them will make a festive and delectable meal.

This chapter is also a reflection of my own culinary journey. Here you'll find iconic recipes such as Refried Beans (page 130), a staple in every Mexican household, and Mexican Rice (page 124), the dish I knew I had to master if I wanted to earn my place as an equal among my aunts in the kitchen. And of course there are Borracho Beans (page 128), which seemed always to be simmering on someone's stove.

Among these are some dishes born of necessity. There are many vegetables I ate so much of as a child I swore I'd never have another. Then I grew up and created recipes like Parmesan Summer Squash (page 146) and Garlic Green Beans (page 141), two examples of easy ways to fall in love again with very familiar ingredients.

broccoli and rice casserole

mexican rice

white rice

black beans

borracho beans

refried beans

baked goat cheese rigatoni

sopa de fideo

lemon fettuccine

tomato-basil spaghetti

spicy roasted brussels sprouts

garlic green beans

brazilian leeks

broiled asparagus

parmesan summer squash

portobello mushrooms

garlic mashed potatoes

veracruz corn

fried plantains

eggplant parmesan

broccoli and rice casserole

This side dish is as easy to put together as it is tasty; my mom made it for us at least once a week. It packs lots of nutrition and flavor into a single dish, it is a very successful way to get kids to eat broccoli, and it is great to eat with so many things. Try it with Tilapia with Citrus-Garlic Sauce (page 74), Lemon Fried Chicken (page 80), or Meat Loaf (page 115). Any amount of butter works here. I tend to use a lot, but feel free to use less.

MAKES 6 TO 8 SERVINGS

- 8 tablespoons (1 stick) unsalted butter, plus more for the baking dish, or as desired
- 3 cups broccoli florets or 1 10-ounce package frozen, chopped broccoli
- 1 cup uncooked long grain white rice
- 1 10.5-ounce can cream of mushroom soup
- 1 cup chopped celery
- ¼ cup chopped onion

1. Preheat the oven to 350°F. Generously butter a 2-quart baking dish and set aside.

2. If using fresh broccoli, place a steamer insert in a lidded saucepan or skillet and add about 2 inches of water to the pan; the water should not come over the holes of the steamer. Place the broccoli in the steamer basket and cover the pan. Bring the water to a boil over high heat. Steam until the broccoli is bright green and tender when pierced with a sharp knife but still crisp, about 5 minutes. If using frozen broccoli, cook it according to package directions.

3. Cook the rice according to package directions. Transfer the cooked broccoli and rice to one large mixing bowl. Add the mushroom soup, celery, and onion and stir until well combined.

4. Transfer to the buttered dish. Dot the top with as much butter as desired and use a fork to gently toss the mixture to barely incorporate the butter. Bake for 30 minutes. Let stand 5 minutes before serving.

mexican rice

Also known as Spanish rice, Mexican Rice is very difficult to make well. Once you add the tomato sauce and water, you can't really touch it or you'll ruin the texture. The hard part is knowing how much spice to add, because the rice won't properly absorb any seasoning once the water is absorbed. This makes it nearly impossible to perfect, and once it is done, it is done.

There's a saying in my family: "When you perfect the rice, you are ready to get married. But not until then." Follow my recipe and your Mexican Rice will be fabulous, too.

Include the chicken to serve it as a main course.

MAKES 4 TO 6 SERVINGS

2 tablespoons vegetable oil

1 large white onion, chopped

5 garlic cloves, minced

1½ cups long grain white rice

2 tablespoons ground cumin

2½ cups Chicken Broth (page 51) or store-bought low sodium chicken broth, plus more as needed

1 14-ounce can tomato sauce

½ teaspoon kosher salt, or to taste

¼ teaspoon ground black pepper, or to taste

6 chicken drumsticks (about 1½ pounds, optional)

1 15-ounce can peas and carrots, drained (optional)

1. In a large skillet, heat the oil over medium heat until hot but not smoking. Add the onion and garlic and cook for 1 minute. Add the rice and cook, stirring occasionally, until the rice is golden brown, 6 to 8 minutes; lower the heat if necessary to keep the rice from burning. Stir in the cumin and cook for 30 seconds. Stir in the chicken broth, tomato sauce, salt, and pepper. Add the chicken, if using, and submerge it under the liquid.

2. Bring to a gentle boil, reduce the heat, cover the pan, and simmer until most of the liquid is absorbed and the rice is cooked, about 30 minutes. Uncover the pan a few times during cooking to check the liquid. Add more chicken broth if the rice starts to burn and sticks to the bottom of the pan. Do not stir during cooking; it causes the rice to break down and become sticky.

3. A minute or two before the rice is done, add the drained peas and carrots, if using.

4. Remove the pan from the heat. Let stand, covered, for at least 10 minutes and up to 1 hour before serving. Taste and season with salt and pepper if necessary. To serve, spoon the rice onto individual plates and place one or two drumsticks on top.

black beans

I always struggled to make perfect black beans, and then my friend from ArtBites (page 63) gave me this recipe, and now my black beans are just as good as my Borracho Beans (page 128)! Black beans are delicious refried (page 130). Black beans, unlike pinto beans, cook more evenly and fall apart less if you skip the soaking.

MAKES 8 TO 10 SERVINGS

1 pound dried black beans

½ yellow onion, chopped

3 garlic cloves, minced

2 tablespoons olive oil

1 chicken bouillon cube

Leaves from 1 bunch of fresh cilantro

Grated or crumbled queso fresco, for serving (optional)

1. Place the beans in a strainer. Pick through and discard any pebbles, debris, or shriveled beans. Rinse the beans well and drain.

2. Place the beans in a Dutch oven or other heavy pot. Add the onion, garlic, oil, bouillon cube, cilantro, and 10 cups of water. Bring to a roaring boil over medium-high heat. Reduce the heat and simmer, partially covered, until the beans are tender, 1½ to 2 hours. Stir the beans every 15 minutes or so to make sure that none are sticking to the bottom of the pot and that the water covers the beans enough to allow them to more or less float freely. Add additional water if necessary. Serve topped with queso fresco, if desired.

FROM AUNT ELSA'S KITCHEN

Dried beans are a great pantry item because they have a long shelf life, but it comes with a caveat: The age of dried beans will affect how long they take to cook. Older beans generally take longer than more recently dried beans. It's generally impossible to tell how old your beans are when you buy them, so be sure to allow for the extra half hour given in the cooking time range.

borracho beans

I love to pull out my slow cooker and let these beans simmer all day, filling the whole house with their amazing aroma. The key to a good bean dish is carefully picking over the dried beans before you cook them, discarding any that are discolored or shriveled.

Use any chunky tomato salsa you like; it adds color and heat, so choose accordingly. I usually save the fat that comes from frying the bacon for these beans and use it to make unbelievably good Refried Beans (page 130).

Sofrito is a combination of aromatic ingredients that are cooked slowly to release their flavor. It is used as the base of many dishes in Latin American and Caribbean cooking. I usually buy prepared sofrito seasoning paste sold in individual packets and located in the spice or Latin food aisle at the grocery store.

MAKES ABOUT 8 CUPS BROTHY BEANS; 6 TO 8 SERVINGS

- 1 pound dried pinto beans
- ¼ pound (about 4 thick strips) bacon, cut into ½-inch pieces
- 1 tablespoon onion powder, plus more if needed
- 1 teaspoon garlic powder, plus more if needed
- ¼ to ½ cup Pace or other chunky salsa
- 1 3.98-ounce package Maggi or other brand sofrito seasoning paste
- Kosher salt and ground black pepper
- 1 bunch of fresh cilantro, leaves chopped, for serving

1. Place the beans in a strainer. Pick through and discard any pebbles, debris, or shriveled beans. Rinse the beans well and drain.

2. To soak the beans overnight, transfer them to a large mixing bowl. Add cold water to cover by 2 inches and set aside to soak for at least 8 hours or overnight.

   Alternatively, to soak the beans more quickly, transfer them to a large saucepan. Add cold water to cover by 2 inches. Bring to a rapid boil over high heat and boil for 2 minutes. Remove the pan from the heat, cover, and let stand 1 hour.

3. Meanwhile, in a small skillet over medium heat, fry the bacon until it's cooked but not crispy. Transfer to a paper towel–lined plate and set aside. If desired, pour off the bacon grease into a small container and reserve for making Refried Beans (page 130).

4. Drain and rinse the soaked beans and place in a Crock-Pot. Add boiling water to cover by 1 inch. Add the onion and garlic powders and cook on high power for 5 to 6 hours, adding more boiling water as necessary to keep the beans submerged and very gently stirring as necessary to keep the beans from sticking to the bottom.

5. About 2 hours into cooking, stir in the salsa and a little more onion and garlic powder, if desired. About 1 hour before the end of cooking, add the reserved bacon, sofrito, 1 teaspoon salt, and a few grindings of black pepper.

6. When the beans are fully cooked, taste and season as necessary with salt and pepper. Ladle the beans into shallow soup bowls, top with cilantro, and serve.

refried beans

In terms of its role in my life, this may well be the most important recipe in this chapter. It is without exaggeration that I say that there were always borracho or refried beans in our house. Barely a day goes by that I don't have beans; my favorite breakfast is refried beans and egg whites. They can replace or be added along with any meat in tacos (page 102), chalupas (page 87), or enchiladas (page 94).

These should be stiff, not runny. Authentic refried beans are made with bacon grease, but vegetable oil is an excellent alternative.

MAKES 4 SERVINGS

2 cups drained Borracho Beans (page 128) or Black Beans (page 127)

1 to 2 tablespoons bean cooking liquid, or as needed (optional)

Reserved bacon grease from Borracho Beans or 1 tablespoon vegetable oil

Grated or crumbled queso fresco, for serving (optional)

1. In the work bowl of a food processor, place the borracho beans. Puree until smooth, adding a little of the bean cooking liquid if necessary to keep the beans from sticking to the blade.

2. In a medium skillet, heat the bacon grease or oil over medium heat until hot. Add the puree and cook, stirring, for 5 minutes. Serve, topped with queso fresco, if desired.

baked goat cheese rigatoni

When I am in Dallas, I make sure to stop in at the Palomino, where the chef puts a unique spin on mac and cheese. He uses rigatoni and goat cheese. It's so creamy and delicious, I finally asked the chef for the recipe so I can make it myself at home! Make sure to use regular, unflavored soft goat cheese.

MAKES 6 TO 8 SERVINGS

Vegetable oil or cooking spray for the baking dish

Kosher salt

8 ounces dried rigatoni pasta

3 tablespoons unsalted butter

3 cups whole milk

¼ cup all-purpose flour

1 cup grated Gruyère cheese

1 cup grated white Cheddar cheese

1 cup grated Parmigiano-Reggiano cheese

½ cup grated Italian fontina cheese

1 4-ounce log soft goat cheese, crumbled

Ground black pepper

1 cup panko

½ cup crumbled goat cheese (2 ounces), for topping

1. Preheat the oven to 350°F. Brush or spray a 2-quart baking dish with vegetable oil or cooking spray.

2. Bring a large pot of salted water to a boil. Add the rigatoni and cook until al dente, 8 to 10 minutes, or according to package directions. Drain the pasta and rinse with cold water to stop the cooking. Drain thoroughly and set aside.

3. Meanwhile, in a medium saucepan over medium heat, melt 1 tablespoon of the butter. Add the milk and heat until hot. Add the flour and stir well so that it doesn't clump. Add ⅔ cup Gruyère, ⅔ cup Cheddar, ½ cup Parmigiano-Reggiano, the fontina, and the log of goat cheese. Stir until the cheese is completely melted and the sauce is smooth. Add salt and pepper to taste. Remove from the heat.

4. Place the panko in a small bowl. Melt the remaining 2 tablespoons of the butter and pour it over the panko. Use a fork to stir until the panko is thoroughly coated in butter. Set aside.

5. In a large mixing bowl, place the noodles and pour over the cheese sauce. Transfer to the prepared baking dish. Scatter over the top the remaining ⅓ cup Gruyère, ⅓ cup Cheddar, ½ cup Parmigiano-Reggiano, and the crumbled goat cheese. Top with the panko mixture.

6. Bake until browned and bubbling, 20 to 25 minutes. Let stand 10 minutes before serving.

sopa de fideo

I call this Mexican spaghetti. In Mexico, sopa de fideo is truly a soup, while fideo seco is much drier. I like a texture between the two. As with Mexican Rice (page 124), the trick is to cook these without touching them very much at all. Any stirring will make the noodles sticky, so when checking the level of the liquid in the pan, just use a long-handled spoon to gently move the noodles aside and check the bottom of the pan. Note that the longer this sits, the more the noodles will absorb the broth.

This is a great method for cooking chicken, so even though I'm serving the noodles only as a side dish, sometimes I take advantage of the simmering pot to cook some chicken for the next day. I add as many drumsticks as possible without crowding, and the well-seasoned broth turns out tender, juicy, and really flavorful chicken every time.

MAKES 4 TO 6 SERVINGS

- 2 tablespoons vegetable oil
- 1 large white onion, chopped
- 5 garlic cloves, minced
- 1 8.8-ounce box fideo or angel hair or vermicelli pasta (see Note)
- 3 to 3½ cups Chicken Broth (page 51) or store-bought low-sodium chicken broth
- 1 14-ounce can tomato sauce
- 2 tablespoons ground cumin
- ½ teaspoon kosher salt, or to taste
- ¼ teaspoon ground black pepper, or to taste
- 6 chicken drumsticks (about 1½ pounds, optional)

1. In a large skillet or Dutch oven (better if using angel hair pasta), heat the oil over medium heat until hot but not smoking. Add the onion and garlic and cook for 1 minute. Add the fideo and cook, stirring occasionally, until the fideo is golden brown but not at all burned, about 2 minutes. Add the chicken broth, tomato sauce, cumin, salt, and pepper and stir once or twice just to blend. Add the chicken, if using, submerging it under the liquid.

2. Bring to a gentle boil, reduce the heat, and cover the pan. Simmer until the liquid is mostly absorbed but there are still small pools of sauce on the surface, and the chicken is cooked, about 30 minutes. Uncover a few times during cooking to check the liquid. Add more broth if the fideo starts to burn and stick to the bottom of the pan, but do not stir vigorously once it comes to a simmer. Stirring causes the fideo to break down and become sticky. Serve hot.

NOTE
If using angel hair, break the nests in half before using. Vermicelli should be broken into 3-inch lengths.

FROM AUNT ELSA'S KITCHEN
The *fideo*—short, dried noodles—can be found in Latin grocery stores, but you can use angel hair or vermicelli instead. If using angel hair, use a bigger pan because the dried noodles take up lots of room before they cook down.

lemon fettuccine

When I go to New York, I often eat at Serafina Restaurant, which makes an amazing lemon spaghetti dish that is so good that I was again inspired to get the recipe. The chef kindly obliged. This version is a little simpler and creamier than the original. As with most other pasta dishes, you want the sauce to be ready before the fettuccine is so that the hot noodles absorb the creamy, lemony sauce (the longer it sits, the less saucy it will be). Note that the broth and cream will need to simmer for a good long time so that they are well reduced. Be sure to grate the lemons before you juice them.

This is wonderful served with grilled chicken brushed with Steak Grill Sauce (page 164).

MAKES 6 TO 8 SERVINGS

- 1 cup Beef Broth (page 114) or store-bought low-sodium beef broth
- 1 cup heavy whipping cream
- Juice from 2 small lemons (about ¼ cup)
- 2 tablespoons unsalted butter
- Grated zest from 2 lemons
- Kosher salt
- 1 pound dried fettuccine

1. In a large skillet, pour the beef broth and whipping cream and stir or whisk together to blend. Bring to a simmer over medium heat. Simmer gently until reduced by a third, to about 1⅓ cups, stirring occasionally, about 20 minutes. Stir in the lemon juice, butter, and lemon zest.

2. Meanwhile, bring a large pot of salted water to a boil. Add the fettuccine to the pot when you're sure the sauce will be ready before the noodles are cooked. Cook the fettuccine until al dente, about 8 minutes or according to package directions.

3. Drain the noodles and immediately add them to the lemon sauce in the skillet. Let stand uncovered 15 minutes so the pasta can absorb the sauce. Serve.

tomato-basil spaghetti

This is one of the dishes I turn to when unexpected guests drop in. The sauce comes together in less time than it takes to boil the water and cook the pasta, but the results are always impressive. Begin the sauce as soon as you put the water on to boil, because it's better if the sauce is ready before the pasta, rather than the other way around.

MAKES 4 TO 6 SERVINGS

Kosher salt

1 pound dried spaghetti or other long pasta

1 tablespoon olive oil

½ small yellow or white onion, chopped

4 garlic cloves, minced

2 bunches of fresh basil, leaves chopped

Ground black pepper to taste

1 14.5-ounce can whole tomatoes with juice

1 8-ounce can tomato sauce

¼ cup grated Parmigiano-Reggiano (about 1 ounce), or to taste, for serving

1 teaspoon dried red pepper flakes or to taste, for serving

1. Bring a large pot of salted water to a boil. Cook the spaghetti to al dente, about 8 minutes or according to package directions.

2. Meanwhile, in a large skillet, heat the oil over medium heat. Add the onion, garlic, half of the basil, and a pinch each of salt and pepper. Cook, stirring occasionally, until translucent, about 5 minutes. Add the tomatoes and the tomato sauce. Bring to a simmer while you break up the tomatoes with the side of a spoon. Simmer gently for 4 minutes. Season with salt and pepper to taste.

3. Drain the pasta and place it in a large serving bowl. Pour over the sauce and add all but a handful of the basil. Toss until the pasta is well coated with sauce. Top with the remaining chopped basil, grated Parmigiano-Reggiano, and dried red pepper flakes. Serve.

spicy roasted brussels sprouts

My family knows that roasting is my favorite way to prepare Brussels sprouts (it's one of my Thanksgiving specialties), so when my sister Emily found a version with kimchi in a magazine, she sent it straight to me. Kimchi, a staple in the Korean diet, is a delicious, tangy, fermented cabbage. It can be found in well-stocked grocery stores and in Korean markets. The flavor of the finished dish really depends on the kimchi, so find one you like.

If you don't like a lot of spice, just roast the Brussels sprouts as directed here and leave out the kimchi. Roasted Brussels sprouts on their own are both sweet and savory.

MAKES 4 SERVINGS

6 cups Brussels sprouts, ends trimmed, halved lengthwise through core

3 tablespoons olive oil

Kosher salt and ground black pepper

1 16-ounce jar medium-spicy kimchi with juice

1. Preheat the oven to 425°F.

2. On a rimmed baking sheet, spread the Brussels sprouts. Drizzle over the oil and season with salt and pepper. Roast, tossing once, until the Brussels sprouts are brown and tender, 20 to 25 minutes.

3. Add the kimchi to the Brussels sprouts and gently toss to combine. Return to the oven and roast until the kimchi is heated through, 1 to 2 minutes. Serve.

garlic green beans

One of my chores when I was a kid was to "top and tail" and remove the strings from the green beans we'd harvested from the garden. The baskets of fresh-picked green beans sometimes seemed endlessly high and I often questioned why I had to go to all that trouble to remove something as harmless as tops and tails. Today I appreciate the simplicity of the task. I love fresh green beans so much that I miss them terribly when they're out of season. You can cook the beans as long as you like; the longer they cook, the sweeter they get.

MAKES 4 TO 6 SERVINGS

Kosher salt to taste

1½ pounds green beans, trimmed and halved if long

3 tablespoons unsalted butter

6 garlic cloves, minced

1. Prepare a large bowl of ice water and bring a large saucepan of lightly salted water to a boil. Add the green beans and cook for 30 seconds. Drain the beans and immediately submerge them in the ice water to stop the cooking. Let the beans sit in the ice water for a couple of minutes, and then drain thoroughly.

2. In a large skillet, heat the butter over medium-low heat. When the butter has melted, add the garlic and cook, stirring occasionally, until softened, 2 to 3 minutes; do not let the garlic brown. Stir in the green beans and cook gently until crisp-tender, 10 to 12 minutes, or until softer to the bite—this is how I like them—20 to 25 minutes. You want to hear a gentle sizzling sound as they cook, but no more than that. Add salt to taste and serve.

FROM AUNT ELSA'S KITCHEN

Placing green vegetables in boiling water for less than a minute and then plunging them into ice water—what professionals call blanching and shocking—keeps them very green and pretty. You can skip this step if you don't have time to wait for the water to boil.

brazilian leeks

I think leeks are underappreciated by most and even intimidating to some people. They are featured in many recipes and restaurant dishes as an aromatic base flavor, but until my Brazilian friend Paolo served them to me this way, I'd never seen them as a proper side dish standing all on their own. They are part of the onion family and, as with onions, slow cooking will bring out their natural sugars. Patience is a real virtue here. Cook them too fast, over heat that's too high, and they will burn. Slow, gentle heat will produce meltingly soft and sweet leeks that can be twirled on a fork like spaghetti. I love these with beef dishes such as Filets Mignons with Sweet Balsamic Reduction (page 108) or Flank Steak with Lime Marinade (page 105).

MAKES 4 TO 6 SERVINGS

4 leeks (white and light green parts only)

4 to 6 tablespoons olive oil

½ tablespoon unsalted butter

Kosher salt and ground black pepper to taste

Sweet Balsamic Reduction (page 165, optional)

1. Trim the leeks and cut them in half lengthwise. Run them under cold running water, using your fingers to gently pull open the layers to rinse away the sand. Shake the excess water from the leeks and use a sharp knife to thinly slice the leeks lengthwise into long, thin strips.

2. In a large skillet, heat the oil and butter over low heat. When the butter is melted, add the leeks. If you cannot add all the leeks at once, add them in batches and use tongs to gently turn them as they cook, bringing the leeks on the bottom of the pan to the top as they reduce in volume to make more room.

3. Once all of the leeks have been added to the pan, cook gently, stirring occasionally, until they are soft enough to be twirled on a fork like spaghetti, 18 to 20 minutes. Add a little more butter or oil if necessary.

4. Serve, drizzling a little reduced balsamic vinegar over each portion, if desired.

broiled asparagus

Broiled asparagus is the vegetable side dish I prepare most often when I'm throwing a big dinner party because it's sophisticated but quick and easy to make. Actually, I prepare it as often as I can, whether I'm having a dinner party or not, because it is my absolute favorite vegetable. I'd eat it for breakfast, lunch, and dinner if I could.

The timing here depends on how thick the asparagus are—they can be pencil thin or super thick. Just pierce them with a knife; when it goes in easily, they're ready to be broiled to get some nice, brown color.

MAKES 6 TO 8 SERVINGS

- 2 bunches asparagus (about 2 pounds), ends trimmed
- 1 tablespoon olive oil
- Kosher salt to taste

1. Position a rack 6 inches from the broiler and preheat the oven to 350°F.

2. Place the asparagus on a rimmed baking sheet. Add the oil and toss to coat. Sprinkle with 1 or 2 pinches of salt. Bake until tender when pierced with the point of a knife, 10 to 20 minutes, depending on the thickness. Turn the broiler to high and broil until browned in spots, 3 to 4 minutes. Watch carefully so the asparagus doesn't burn. Serve.

ANOTHER REASON TO GO GREEN

I love all vegetables, but especially green ones, which is why I use them in so many of my recipes. Asparagus, Brussels sprouts, broccoli, green peppers, and, especially, leafy greens like spinach are packed with antioxidants and fiber—and taste amazing.

---

parmesan summer squash

When I was a kid, my mom cooked squash all the time because it grew (abundantly!) in our garden. I admit I had to learn to love it, and this is one of the ways I learned. Slow cooking and a touch of Parmesan bring out the natural sweetness of the squash. It's also beautiful; the green and yellow colors really pop off the plate.

**MAKES 4 TO
6 SERVINGS**

2 tablespoons olive oil

1 small white onion, chopped

2 medium yellow summer squash (about 1 pound), thinly sliced

2 medium zucchini (about 1 pound), thinly sliced

½ teaspoon kosher salt, or to taste

Ground black pepper to taste

¼ cup grated Parmesan cheese (about 1 ounce)

1. In a large skillet with a tight-fitting lid, heat the oil over medium heat. Add the onion and cook, stirring occasionally, just until tender and fragrant, about 3 minutes.

2. Add the summer squash, zucchini, and salt. It may be necessary to let some of the squash and zucchini cook down a little before you can add all of them to the pan. Stir well, cover, and cook for 10 minutes, stirring occasionally. Check the texture: If you prefer a little more cooked, return the pan to the heat and cook, covered, for a few minutes longer.

3. Remove from the heat and add salt to taste and several grindings of black pepper. Transfer the squash to a serving bowl and sprinkle the Parmesan on top. Serve.

portobello mushrooms

Portobello mushrooms are so meaty and flavorful that many of my vegetarian friends prepare and eat them the way I do steak—throwing them on the grill and making a main course of them. For my part, I'll take the steak *and* the portobellos, ideally prepared the way they are here: cooked simply so that their natural qualities can shine.

MAKES 4 SERVINGS

3 tablespoons unsalted butter or olive oil, or as needed for grilling

4 large portobello mushroom caps (about 12 ounces), sliced ¾ inch thick, or prepackaged portobello slices

Kosher salt to taste

1. If sautéing, in a large skillet heat the butter or oil over medium heat. Add the mushrooms to the pan and cook until lightly browned, 6 to 8 minutes. Flip the slices over and brown the other side, 6 to 8 minutes.

   If grilling, spray a grill grate or grill pan with cooking spray or brush with olive oil. Prepare a medium-high grill or place the grill pan over medium-high heat. Add the mushroom slices and grill until softened and grill marks are clearly visible, 4 to 6 minutes per side.

2. Sprinkle with salt and serve.

garlic mashed potatoes

An electric stand mixer makes mashed potatoes dangerously easy to prepare. You may find yourself eating them every night! Just be sure to leave them a little chunky: If you overmix them, they'll become gluey. I love to eat these as a side with just about anything, especially Chicken Fried Steak with White Gravy (page 106). They're so good that sometimes I even serve them as an appetizer, spooned into cocktail glasses and topped with a sprinkling of chopped fresh chives.

**MAKES ABOUT
6 SERVINGS**

4 large russet potatoes (about 3 pounds), peeled and chopped into roughly 2-inch dice

2 tablespoons kosher salt

4 tablespoons (½ stick) unsalted butter, or more to taste

1 head garlic, cloves peeled and minced

½ cup milk, warmed

Ground black pepper to taste

1. Place the potatoes in a large saucepan. Add the salt and cold water to cover by 1 inch. Bring to a boil over high heat. Reduce the heat to a gentle boil and cook until the potatoes fall apart when poked with a fork, 10 to 15 minutes. Drain the potatoes well and transfer them to the work bowl of an electric stand mixer fitted with the whisk attachment.

2. Meanwhile, melt 2 tablespoons of the butter in a skillet over medium-low heat. Add the garlic and cook gently, stirring occasionally, until softened and very lightly browned, 3 to 5 minutes. Add the garlic-butter mixture to the bowl with the potatoes. Add the remaining 2 tablespoons butter, the warm milk, and the pepper. Mix on medium-low speed until creamy but still chunky, no more than 1 minute. Do not overmix or the potatoes will become gluey. Serve.

veracruz corn

One bite and you'll know why this sweet and spicy corn is one of the most popular dishes at my Beso restaurants. The smoky Chipotle Aïoli (page 162) was created especially for this and it absolutely makes the dish. You can pour it on heavy, like they do at the restaurant, or pour it on lighter, like I do here, but don't skip it! The optional tortilla strips add crunch and heft. To cook the corn, grill or boil it.

MAKES 4 SERVINGS

4 ears of corn, husked

Cooking spray, if using the grill

1 teaspoon vegetable oil, plus more as needed

5 corn tortillas, cut into ¼-inch slices (optional)

¼ cup finely chopped red onion

2 jalapeños, stemmed, seeded, and finely chopped

Kosher salt and ground black pepper

2 to 4 tablespoons Chipotle Aïoli (page 162) or to taste

1 cup grated or crumbled queso fresco (about 4 ounces)

1. If grilling the corn, coat the grill grate with cooking spray and prepare a medium-high grill. Brush the corn with oil and place it on the grill. Cook, turning, until the corn is evenly cooked and browned in spots, 5 to 7 minutes.

   If boiling the corn, bring a large pot of water to a boil. Add the corn, cover, and remove from the heat. Let stand 3 to 5 minutes. Drain well.

2. When the corn is cool enough to handle, cut it from the cob and set aside.

3. If using the tortillas, line a baking sheet or large plate with paper towels. In a large skillet, heat 1 cup of the vegetable oil over medium-high heat until shimmery and hot but not smoking. Add a handful or two of tortilla strips—they can be touching but not overlapping—and fry just until lightly browned around the edges, about 45 seconds. Transfer the strips to the paper towel–lined baking sheet, tossing and moving them around so they take on squiggly shapes as they cool and harden. Continue in batches until all the tortilla strips are fried, adding more oil to the pan if necessary. Set aside.

(recipe continues)

4. In a small, preferably ovenproof, skillet, heat 1 teaspoon of the oil over medium heat. Add the onion and jalapeño and cook, stirring occasionally, until softened and fragrant, 2 to 3 minutes. Add the corn and tortillas, if using, and toss until warmed through. Add a pinch each of salt and pepper, or to taste. If necessary, transfer to a small, ovenproof dish.

5. Drizzle the aïoli on top and sprinkle with the cheese.

6. Place an oven rack 6 inches from the broiler and turn the broiler to high. Place the skillet or dish under the broiler and cook until browned and bubbling, about 5 minutes. Watch carefully so it does not burn. Serve.

QUESO FRESCO

Queso fresco, or "fresh cheese," is a mild, salty cheese used widely in Mexican cooking. It has a crumbly texture; some brands are more easily crumbled with your hands than grated. Sprinkled over hot food, it softens beautifully and becomes creamy rather than stringy, like some other cheeses. Queso fresco is widely available, and grocery stores that sell a wide selection of Latin food will usually have at least a couple of brands to choose from. Try a few to find one you like; my favorite brand is Cacique Ranchero. Tightly wrapped, queso fresco will last up to 2 weeks in the refrigerator.

fried plantains

This is the best way I know to prepare ripe plantains, a classic Caribbean dish that is served with Crock-Pot Cuban Ropa Vieja (page 113). Ripe plantains are so sweet that they can actually be prepared this way and served over vanilla ice cream. But don't let that sweetness intimidate you. Sweet often complements savory, and these are especially wonderful with hearty stews and grilled red meat. If the plantains are very mushy, they'll need to be sliced thicker and will cook faster because they have more sugars, which caramelize really quickly in the hot oil.

MAKES 4 TO 6 SERVINGS

5 extremely ripe plantains (peels should be black with no yellow spots)

½ cup vegetable oil, or as needed

Kosher salt to taste

1. Working with one plantain at a time, use a sharp knife to cut off both ends. Run the tip of the knife down the full length of the plantain 2 or 3 times, cutting through the thick skin but not into the plantain. Work the peel off with your hands. Repeat with the remaining plantains. Slice the peeled plantains at a diagonal into thick slices.

2. Line a baking sheet or large platter with paper towels. In a large skillet, heat the oil over medium heat until shimmery and hot but not smoking. Add as many plantain slices as will fit without crowding and cook until browned, 3 to 4 minutes. Adjust the heat as necessary so the oil is bubbling happily around the slices. Turn the slices over and cook until browned on the other side, 3 to 4 minutes. Transfer to the paper towels to drain, and immediately sprinkle with salt to taste. Repeat with the remaining slices until all are cooked and salted, adding more oil to the pan as needed. Serve hot.

FROM AUNT ELSA'S KITCHEN
It can be hard to find black plantains at the store, since once they're black, they're so ripe that they don't have much shelf life left. It's better to buy them when they're still a little yellow and let them finish ripening at home. Placing them in a paper bag will speed up the process.

eggplant parmesan

I first learned this dish for my good friend Lake Bell, a vegetarian I really wanted to have over for dinner. When I don't have vegetarians at the table, I serve this as a side dish, but even my meat-loving friends like it so much that sometimes they make it their whole dinner with a salad of romaine lettuce and Grey Moss Inn White French Dressing (page 160).

MAKES 6 TO 8 SERVINGS

- ½ cup vegetable oil, or as needed
- 1 large eggplant (about 1½ pounds)
- 2 large eggs
- ½ cup Italian-style dry bread crumbs
- 1¼ cups grated Parmesan cheese
- 4 cups Beef Bolognese (page 111) or 1 26-ounce jar store-bought bolognese or marinara
- 8 ounces mozzarella cheese, thinly sliced

1. Preheat the oven to 350°F. Lightly brush or spray a 9 × 13-inch baking dish with vegetable oil.

2. Wash the eggplant, but do not peel it. Cut it crosswise in ¼-inch-thick slices. In a shallow dish or pie plate, lightly beat the eggs. In another shallow dish or pie plate, combine the bread crumbs with ½ cup Parmesan cheese, and stir with a fork until well combined.

3. Working with one eggplant slice at a time, coat it on both sides with the egg and allow the excess to drip off. Place it in the bread crumbs, and coat on both sides. Transfer to a platter or baking sheet.

4. Line a baking sheet with paper towels. In a large skillet, heat 2 table-spoons of the oil over medium-high heat until shimmery and hot but not smoking. Add as many slices of eggplant as can fit in a single layer; do not crowd the pan. Cook until golden brown and crisp on both sides, 1 to 2 minutes per side. Transfer the eggplant slices to the prepared baking sheet. Repeat with the remaining slices, adding more oil as needed.

5. Meanwhile, pour the Bolognese in a small saucepan; if using jarred sauce, add a little water to the jar. Close the jar and shake it to loosen the sauce stuck to the sides of the jar. Add the water to the saucepan. Over medium heat bring the sauce just to boiling. Cover, set aside, and keep warm.

6. Arrange half of the eggplant slices along the bottom of the prepared baking dish. Top the eggplant with half of the warm sauce. Arrange half of the mozzarella slices on top and sprinkle with half of the remaining Parmesan cheese. Arrange the remaining eggplant slices over the cheese. Cover with the remaining meat sauce, mozzarella, and Parmesan.

7. Bake, uncovered, until the cheese is melted and slightly browned, 25 to 30 minutes. Let stand 5 minutes before serving.

FROM AUNT ELSA'S KITCHEN
For a pretty presentation, set aside half of the most uniformly sized eggplant slices for the top layer. Use the rest for the bottom layer that no one can see.

A LOVE LETTER
One of my greatest joys is a beautiful and well-organized produce section, where everything is in its place, fresh, and easy to find. I'd like to take a moment to write a love letter to all the grocery store managers who oversee these wonderful produce sections. I am extremely grateful when all the signs are correct and readable so that when I am searching for an unfamiliar ingredient, I can find it easily. I know that others have had an experience like I did the first time I went to the store to buy rhubarb to make a Strawberry Rhubarb Pie (page 198). Being from Texas, I had no idea what rhubarb looked like or where to begin to search for it in the produce section. I didn't know whether it was a fruit or a vegetable; big or small; green, pink, or blue! In the end, I simply asked a clerk, which is something I enthusiastically encourage you to do. Don't be afraid to ask! Those people lurking by the lemons are there to help. They not only know where things are, they should also know what's in the back waiting to be brought out and what they've ordered for tomorrow. I am rarely more frustrated than when I come into a store where the produce section is in disarray and the folks working there seem as confused as the customers surely are. Please, conscientious produce managers everywhere, remember that the produce in the store was grown and harvested by human beings, and it's vital to treat this food with a respect worthy of the hard labor that made it possible.

dressings & sauces

In my family, no one would ever consider buying something that could be easily and inexpensively made at home. I still remember my grandmother tossing together green salads with nothing more than some vegetable oil, white vinegar, and maybe a little salt. I also remember that my *abuela*'s salads were the best I ever tasted. When I learned how to make my own dressings at home, I figured out that, especially when I expanded beyond plain vegetable oil and white vinegar, they tasted much better than anything I could buy. Best yet, they store really well, so you can make a batch for your salad one night and then save the rest in the refrigerator to use all week long on tossed salads or to marinate meat.

Sauces, on the other hand, were not part of our food culture. My dad wouldn't even allow us to have ketchup on french fries! I spent years as an adult believing that sauces were universally heavy and diminished the flavor of whatever they were served with.

While traveling and eating through Europe, however, I learned that rather than mask flavor, good sauces can actually bring out the taste of the food they're served with. Over time I've discovered or developed the recipes in this chapter. They offer great flavor and, just as important, versatility. They can be served with vegetables, fish, poultry, or meat. And while I haven't embraced soaking all my food in sauce, I now happily prepare and enjoy many sauces—and eat ketchup with my fries!

---

balsamic vinaigrette

lemon garlic dressing

grey moss inn white french dressing

buttermilk dressing

chipotle aïoli

steak grill sauce

bbq sauce

sweet balsamic reduction

citrus-garlic sauce

lemon butter sauce

shiitake-wine sauce

balsamic vinaigrette

This vinaigrette is excellent on just about any green salad. I especially like it on butterhead lettuce, oak leaf, and other delicate greens. Sweet-and-tangy balsamic vinegar is the star here, so choose one that is good quality.

MAKES ABOUT 1 CUP

- 6 tablespoons balsamic vinegar
- 2 small shallots, finely minced

  Kosher salt and ground black pepper to taste
- ⅔ cup extra-virgin olive oil

1. In a small bowl, whisk together the vinegar, shallots, salt, and pepper. Whisking constantly, add the oil in a slow, steady stream and continue to whisk until well blended.

2. Use at once or store in a tightly covered container in the refrigerator for up to 1 week.

lemon garlic dressing

Few ingredients awaken the taste buds the way fresh lemon does. This dressing has a clean, pure flavor perfectly suited to a light salad of tossed greens. It may also have some magical qualities—it's the one dressing that gets my nieces to eat salad! It can also be used as a marinade for grilled chicken, shrimp, or pork.

MAKES ABOUT 1½ CUPS

- Juice of 4 small lemons (about ½ cup)
- 2 teaspoons distilled white vinegar
- 2 teaspoons Dijon mustard
- 2 garlic cloves, minced

  Kosher salt and ground black pepper to taste
- ¾ cup extra-virgin olive oil

1. In a medium mixing bowl, whisk together the lemon juice, vinegar, mustard, garlic, salt, and pepper until well blended. Whisking constantly, add the oil in a slow, steady stream and continue to whisk until well blended.

2. Use at once or store in a tightly covered container in the refrigerator for up to 1 week.

grey moss inn
white french dressing

I am lucky to live near the Grey Moss Inn, one of the most beautiful restaurants in San Antonio, which also has the most amazing wine list in the area. I love to eat there whenever I can, and this dressing is one of the reasons. After tasting it the first time, I once again found myself in a restaurant kitchen asking for the recipe. The chef graciously agreed. Try it tossed with tender romaine hearts, or spoon over asparagus (page 145), tomatoes, or steamed green beans.

**MAKES ABOUT
1¾ CUPS**

1 large white onion, peeled and quartered

6 small garlic cloves

¼ cup mayonnaise

Juice from 2 limes (about ¼ cup juice)

3 tablespoons red wine vinegar

½ teaspoon kosher salt

½ teaspoon ground white pepper

1. In the work bowl of a food processor, place the onion and garlic. Process until pureed, scraping down the sides of the work bowl once or twice. Transfer to a medium mixing bowl and add the mayonnaise, lime juice, vinegar, salt, and pepper. Whisk together until thoroughly blended.

2. Use at once or store in a tightly covered container in the refrigerator for up to 1 week.

buttermilk dressing

This sweet, herby dressing has great texture and bold flavors, and it's delicious with hardier greens such as baby spinach and romaine. It's also excellent as a sandwich condiment and drizzled over grilled chicken.

MAKES ABOUT 2 CUPS

- ½ cup extra-virgin olive oil
- ½ cup reduced-fat mayonnaise
- ½ cup buttermilk
- 2 tablespoons grainy mustard, such as moutarde de Meaux
- 2 tablespoons red wine vinegar
- 1 teaspoon sugar
- 2 tablespoons capers, rinsed and chopped
- 2 tablespoons minced shallots
- 2 teaspoons chopped fresh oregano
- 1 teaspoon chopped fresh basil
- 1 teaspoon chopped fresh tarragon
- Kosher salt to taste
- Hot red pepper sauce to taste

1. In a medium mixing bowl, whisk together the olive oil, mayonnaise, buttermilk, mustard, vinegar, sugar, capers, shallots, oregano, basil, and tarragon until well blended. Add kosher salt and red pepper sauce to taste.

2. Use at once or store in a tightly covered container in the refrigerator for up to 1 week.

FROM AUNT ELSA'S KITCHEN
To store fresh herbs, place them in a zip-top plastic bag with a damp paper towel. Seal the top and place in the crisper drawer in the refrigerator. The dampness will help keep them fresh longer.

chipotle aïoli

Chipotles in adobo are smoked jalapeños in seasoned tomato sauce sold in cans available at most grocery stores. When you make this, it looks like it won't work with such a small amount in the food processor, but once the oil is added it will come together. Most important is that you add the oil very slowly, just a few drops at first. If too much goes in at once, the sauce will separate into a gloppy mess and you'll have to start all over again. This smoky aïoli is well worth the effort: The heavenly VeraCruz Corn (page 151) depends on it. And drizzle it over the Flautas (page 93) in place of the tomatillo-avocado sauce.

MAKES ABOUT ½ CUP

- 1 large egg yolk
- 1 teaspoon Dijon mustard
- 2 teaspoons fresh lemon juice
- 1 small garlic clove, minced
- ½ cup canola oil
- 2 teaspoons minced chipotle in adobo sauce
- Kosher salt to taste

1. In the work bowl of a food processor, place the egg yolk, mustard, lemon juice, and garlic. Process until blended. With the food processor running, add the oil just a few drops at a time. When the mixture begins to resemble mayonnaise (this will take a while because you're adding the oil so slowly), pour in the remaining oil in a very fine, slow stream.

2. If making the aïoli to be drizzled over VeraCruz corn or a salad, thin it if necessary by adding water 1 tablespoon at a time until it is pourable. If using as a condiment to be spread or dolloped, it may not need any thinning.

3. Add the chipotle and process until well blended. Add several pinches of salt to taste. Use at once or store in a tightly covered container in the refrigerator for 2 to 3 days.

FROM AUNT ELSA'S KITCHEN
It's unusual to use a full can of chipotle in adobo in a single recipe, but leaving them in the can in the fridge for too long can impart an unpleasant metallic taste. To store the chipotles in adobo, place one or two chipotles and a spoonful of sauce in a snack-size zip-top bag and store in the freezer. This makes it easy to pull out only as much as you need, when you need it.

steak grill sauce

These are ingredients I always have on hand, so this grill sauce is easy to pull together in just a few minutes to add luscious flavor to grilled steak or ribs. When I have a little more time, I make it an hour or two in advance and use half to marinate the meat before grilling and the other half to brush on while grilling.

MAKES ABOUT ⅔ CUP

¼ cup olive oil

2 tablespoons Worcestershire sauce

2 tablespoons soy sauce

2 tablespoons ketchup

¾ teaspoon sugar

¾ teaspoon kosher salt

1. In a small bowl, whisk together the oil, Worcestershire sauce, soy sauce, ketchup, sugar, and salt. Brush on steaks frequently during grilling.

2. Use at once or store in the refrigerator in a tightly covered container for up to 1 week.

bbq sauce

My sister Esmeralda uses this on her excellent BBQ Chicken Pizza (page 91), and it's also good brushed on burgers on the grill. Dried barbecue seasoning can be found in the spice aisle at the grocery store.

MAKES ABOUT ½ CUP

½ cup ketchup

1 teaspoon distilled vinegar

1 garlic clove, pressed, or ½ teaspoon garlic powder

1½ tablespoons barbecue seasoning

1. In a small mixing bowl, place the ketchup, vinegar, garlic, and barbecue seasoning. Stir until very well combined.

2. Use at once or store in the refrigerator in a tightly covered container for up to 1 week.

sweet balsamic reduction

This makes a wonderful sweet-tart condiment with caramelized, almost molasses, under-tones. It lasts for at least two weeks in the fridge and is amazing drizzled over creamy, mild ingredients such as avocado slices or soft goat cheese spread on crackers. It's especially good over filet mignon (page 108) and Brazilian Leeks (page 142), which in fact go beautifully together.

MAKES 3 TO 4 TABLESPOONS

½ cup good-quality balsamic vinegar

5 teaspoons sugar

1. In a small saucepan, place the balsamic vinegar and the sugar. Heat over medium-low heat and stir until the sugar is dissolved. Bring to a simmer and simmer until the vinegar is reduced to 3 to 4 tablespoons, is the consistency of warmed honey, and has a rich, caramelized sweet-tart flavor, about 10 minutes.

2. Serve warm or at room temperature. Store in a tightly covered container in the refrigerator for up to 2 weeks.

citrus-garlic sauce

MAKES ABOUT ½ CUP

3 tablespoons unsalted butter

4 garlic cloves, minced

Grated zest from 1 lemon

Grated zest from 1 lime

Juice from 2 small lemons (about 4 tablespoons)

Juice from 1 lime (about 2 tablespoons)

Kosher salt to taste

3 tablespoons chopped fresh basil

This fabulous citrus sauce comes together in minutes. It is an elegant addition that brightens any fish dish, or try it on chicken cutlets.

1. In a small skillet over medium heat, melt the butter. Add the garlic and cook, stirring, until fragrant, about 30 seconds.

2. Add the lemon and lime zest and juice and a pinch of salt. Cook for 1 to 2 minutes.

3. Add the basil and cook for 1 minute. Remove from the heat and serve over fish or chicken.

lemon butter sauce

I tasted this sauce for the first time in Normandy, France. It was served over Dover sole (page 70) and after I'd eaten it I made my way directly to the tiny kitchen. There the chef rattled off the recipe in rapid French while I frantically scribbled whatever I could understand and asked him questions in my pigeon French. I did, at least, grasp that success depends on using very cold Normandy or European butter (page 25)—believe me, I've tried it with ordinary supermarket butter and it's not at all the same. This is as good over delicate flat fish as it is over richer salmon.

MAKES ABOUT ½ CUP

- 2 tablespoons fresh lemon juice (from 1 small lemon)
- 8 tablespoons cold, unsalted Normandy butter, cut into 8 equal pieces

1. In a small skillet, pour the lemon juice and bring to a boil over medium heat. Whisking constantly, add the cold butter 1 tablespoon at a time. Make sure the butter is very cold when added and fully melted before adding the next tablespoon or else the sauce will simply separate into plain melted butter.

2. When all the butter is incorporated, turn off the heat and pour into a glass measuring cup or gravy boat.

3. Serve warm.

shiitake-wine sauce

This intense wine sauce is delicious and pours lusciously. I think up excuses to serve this as often as I can, on chicken (page 83), filet mignon (page 108), or steak. This is the one sauce that I really love to eat in abundance, so this recipe makes a generous amount—spoon a little on top of each serving and pass the rest at the table.

MAKES ABOUT 2 CUPS

- 1 tablespoon unsalted butter
- 2 tablespoons olive oil
- ½ pound fresh shiitake mushrooms, stems removed, caps thinly sliced
- 2 large shallots (about 4 ounces), finely chopped
- Kosher salt and ground black pepper
- 1½ cups dry red wine
- 1¼ cups Beef Broth (page 114) or store-bought low-sodium beef broth
- 1 tablespoon low-sodium soy sauce
- 1 tablespoon Worcestershire sauce
- 2 teaspoons cornstarch
- 1 tablespoon chopped fresh thyme leaves

1. In a nonstick skillet over medium heat, melt the butter and add the oil. Add the shiitakes, shallots, and a pinch each of salt and pepper. Cook, stirring, until softened, about 4 minutes.

2. Add 1 cup of the wine and ¾ cup of the beef broth and bring to a boil. Reduce the heat and simmer for 5 minutes, stirring often.

3. Use a slotted spoon to transfer the mushrooms to a small bowl. Increase the heat to high and boil the wine mixture until reduced to ½ cup, 10 to 15 minutes.

4. In a small bowl combine the soy sauce, Worcestershire, and cornstarch. Stir well until the cornstarch has dissolved. Pour into the wine mixture along with the remaining ½ cup wine and ½ cup beef broth. Bring to a boil and simmer for 3 minutes.

5. Return the mushrooms to the skillet along with the chopped thyme and boil for 1 minute, stirring constantly, until the wine mixture has thickened. Remove from the heat and serve.

6. Store in a tightly covered container in the refrigerator for up to 1 week.

tortillas, biscuits & quick breads

Tortillas were to my Mexican-American family what sandwich bread is to most other American families: indispensable. Before school I caught the bus in front of Aunt Edna's house. Every morning she made fresh flour tortillas and spread butter on them for us to take on the bus to school. You can imagine the ridicule I endured as one of the only Mexicans attending the school, jumping on the bus with a tortilla in her hand. I might as well have been wearing a sombrero! But it didn't matter to me. Those tortillas were the reason I got out of bed in the morning. To this day my mouth waters just thinking about them.

The truth is that Aunt Edna made the best tortillas in the family, although she never had the satisfaction of hearing us say it out loud because my other aunts and my mom would have been too mad! But we all knew it, and I begged her to show me how to make them. Even today, I love making Aunt Edna's Homemade Flour Tortillas (page 171) for my family and friends. Everyone loves them!

The other tortilla recipe in this chapter is for Corn Tortillas (page 174), a more enduring tradition than even Aunt Edna's flour tortillas. Corn tortillas predate the arrival of Europeans to the New World by thousands of years.

This chapter is rounded out by a handful of timeless classics of more recent origin. No Southern cook's recipe box is complete without dependable recipes for both biscuits (page 177) and corn bread (page 181).

Finally, in a house like mine where nothing ever went to waste, sometimes the intoxicating smell of sweet bread baking in the oven would tell us that a bunch of bananas had turned too brown or the crop of pumpkins had overwhelmed our pantry.

---

aunt edna's homemade flour tortillas

corn tortillas

aunt elsa's buttermilk biscuits

banana bread

pumpkin bread

corn bread

aunt edna's homemade flour tortillas

There are as many different styles of tortillas as there are regions in the parts of the world where they are eaten. I make tortillas like the ones I grew up eating in my Aunt Edna's kitchen in Texas: thick, fluffy, and addictive! This dough can be used to make them any way you like: small or large, thick or thin. With practice, you'll get more efficient and turn into a one-person assembly line: cooking one tortilla while you roll out another.

   Nothing is better to sop up the creamy gravy of Aunt Didi's Carne Guisada (page 107). Or eat them warm, straight off the *comal* (a flat griddle, page 173) and spread with butter. I still love them for breakfast, these days usually with beans rolled up inside.

**MAKES 12 SMALL OR
8 LARGE TORTILLAS**

2½ cups all-purpose flour, plus more for kneading and rolling

1 teaspoon table salt

1 teaspoon baking powder

⅓ cup vegetable shortening, cold and cut up into pieces

¾ cup hot water, plus more as needed

1. In a large mixing bowl, place the flour, salt, and baking powder. Whisk together until well blended. Add the shortening and use your fingers or a pastry blender to cut it into the flour until the mixture resembles coarse meal.

2. Slowly add the water, mixing it in with your fingers a little at a time. Turn the dough out onto a surface and knead until soft, 3 to 4 minutes. Place the dough in a clean, large bowl, cover with a towel, and let rest for 20 minutes.

3. Divide the dough into equal portions and roll each portion into a ball. Place the balls on a baking sheet or platter, cover with a towel, and let rest 20 minutes.

4. On a lightly floured surface, use a rolling pin (*palota*) to roll one ball at a time into an evenly thick round; roll it to about ⅛ inch thick for thick, chewy tortillas or as thin as you like. It is more important that the round be evenly thick than a perfect circle, but there is a good method to getting a good, round shape: Place the ball on the lightly floured surface in front of you and flatten it slightly with your palm or the rolling pin. Place your rolling pin at the center of the round and roll once straight up and then straight down. Do not allow your

(recipe continues)

tortillas, biscuits & quick breads   171

rolling pin to roll right off the edges; just roll up to the edges, not off them. Lift the round and give it a quarter turn. Repeat the rolling and quarter turning until the round is the desired size and thickness. Place the rolled-out tortilla on a baking sheet or large platter and cover with a damp cloth while you roll out the remaining tortillas. Once you have the hang of it, you'll be able to roll and cook at the same time.

5. Heat a *comal* over medium heat until hot. Place a tortilla on the *comal* and cook until the underside is brown in spots, the tortilla has risen slightly, and the surface is dotted with air bubbles, 1 to 1½ minutes. Flip the tortilla and cook until that side is browned in spots (usually where the bubbles were), 1 to 1½ minutes. For best results, do not flip the tortilla more than once. Transfer the tortilla to a tortilla warmer or place on a platter and cover with a cloth napkin while you cook the remaining tortillas. Serve warm.

FROM AUNT ELSA'S KITCHEN

Try to flip flour and corn tortillas (page 174) only once; flipping them back and forth makes the tortillas tough. • Wrapped tightly, flour tortillas can be stored for several days in the refrigerator. Reheat them on the *comal* just before serving.

ESSENTIAL EQUIPMENT FOR TORTILLAS: TORTILLA PRESS, *COMAL,* AND TORTILLA WARMER

A tortilla press is essential for making Corn Tortillas (page 174) and Tostones (page 34). It is made from two round, heavy plates. One sits solidly on the counter and the other, attached to the first by a hinge, is pushed down over the first using the leverage of the handle. It's a beautifully simple design that hasn't been improved by the introduction of new technologies or materials. Buy the heaviest one you can find; I like cast iron. The weight helps do the pressing for you. Don't buy nonstick or electric presses. Be sure to line both sides of the press with wax paper or plastic wrap or the tortilla will stick to it. Tortilla presses can not only be found at kitchen supply retailers, department stores, and online, but they can also often be found for half the price in grocery stores catering to a Latin clientele.

A *comal* is a flat, heavy griddle—again, I prefer cast iron—crucial for cooking tortillas. They are widely available at big box and department stores and well worth their very reasonable price. They're sturdy enough to last decades and are great for searing meat and making quesadillas, panini, and grilled cheese.

Unlike the tortilla press and *comal,* a lidded tortilla warmer is not crucial for producing the most successful tortillas possible. You can certainly place cooked, warm tortillas on a platter and cover them with a clean, cloth napkin or pretty kitchen towel. But tortilla warmers are fun and often beautiful. I love to collect them, in fact, and have a large assortment of warmers made from cloth, ceramic, terra-cotta, and porcelain. I love to present everything I serve in an attractive way, and tortilla warmers look lovely on the table while actually doing the useful job of keeping my fresh tortillas moist and warm!

corn tortillas

The corn tortilla was first made many thousands of years ago. Today it usually begins with masa harina, a powdery meal made from fresh corn dough that has been dried and ground to a powder. Full of sweet and earthy corn flavor, homemade corn tortillas are very different from store-bought. The moment you pull off the lid from the tortilla warmer or the napkin covering a basket of warm tortillas, a sweet, corn aroma fills the air. Serve these with Chili-Rubbed Skirt Steak Tacos (page 102) or in any recipe that calls for corn tortillas.

MAKES ABOUT 16 TORTILLAS

2 cups masa harina

¼ teaspoon table salt

1¼ cups hot water, plus more as needed

1. In a large bowl, place the masa harina, salt, and hot water. Mix with a spoon or your hands until a soft but not sticky dough forms, about 2 minutes. If the mixture seems too dry when a small handful is squeezed together, add more water one tablespoon at a time.

2. Scoop out pieces of dough and roll them into balls about the size of a Ping-Pong ball. Place the balls on a baking sheet or large platter and cover them with a damp cloth while you work to keep the dough moist.

3. Line a tortilla press with plastic wrap. Set the press next to the stovetop.

4. Preheat a *comal*, skillet, or griddle over medium-high heat until hot.

5. Working with one ball at a time, place each ball on the press between the sheets of plastic wrap. Use the handle to press and flatten the ball into a disk 5 to 6 inches in diameter. Open the press and peel the tortilla off the plastic wrap.

6. Place the tortilla on the skillet and cook until the underside is browned in spots, about 1 minute. Flip the tortilla and cook the other side 1 minute; the tortilla should puff up in the center.

7. Transfer to a cloth-lined basket and continue pressing and cooking tortillas, stacking them and keeping them covered, until all are cooked. Serve warm.

aunt elsa's buttermilk biscuits

Aunt Elsa always had a huge container of biscuit mix in her freezer, so whenever she needed biscuits she would scoop some out, add water or buttermilk, and have a batch baking in just a few minutes. When I was a kid, it seemed like magic. I was an adult when she brought me my first container of mix and I realized that this magic powder was in fact her own version of instant biscuit mix! Sometimes I mix up 3 or 4 times the recipe and store it in the freezer so I, too, can make magic biscuits. Tender and flaky, they are best straight out of the oven. The baked biscuits don't store well, but I've rarely had any leftovers!

MAKES ABOUT 2 DOZEN

- 5 cups all-purpose flour, plus more for kneading and rolling
- 3 tablespoons baking powder
- 1 heaping tablespoon sugar
- 1 teaspoon table salt
- 1 cup very cold shortening, cut into ½-inch pieces
- 2 cups buttermilk, plus more as needed
- Butter, for serving (optional)
- Honey, for serving (optional)

1. Position a rack in the upper third of the oven and preheat the oven to 425°F.

2. In a large bowl, place the flour, baking powder, sugar, and salt. Whisk together until well blended. Add the shortening and use your hands or a pastry blender to very quickly blend it into the flour until there are some pieces the size of small peas and some twice that size. If desired, you can transfer the mixture to a tightly sealed container and freeze until needed.

3. Add the buttermilk at once and stir just until blended into a sticky dough; if it seems dry, add more buttermilk 1 tablespoon at a time.

4. Turn the dough out onto a lightly floured surface and knead with your hands 5 to 10 times, just until a ball forms. Use a floured rolling pin to roll out the dough ½ inch thick. Use a 2- or 2½-inch biscuit cutter to cut out as many biscuits as you can and transfer them to an ungreased cookie sheet; place them close together so that all of the biscuits will fit on one sheet. Gather the scraps together into a ball (handling the dough as little as possible). Roll it out to ½ inch thick and cut out as many biscuits as you can. Place them on the sheet; discard the remaining scraps.

5. Bake until puffed and golden on top, 15 to 18 minutes. Serve hot, and spread with butter and honey if desired.

banana bread

Nothing ever went to waste in my house. If bananas got too brown, we knew banana bread was on its way. In fact, I couldn't wait for the bananas to go brown! I happily made my family's recipe for years, until the day I tasted my friend Teri Hatcher's banana bread on the set of *Desperate Housewives.* She's our unofficial on-set baker, and her philosophy on banana bread is "the more booze, the better the bread." This version is like using bananas Foster to make banana bread. The flavor is fantastic and it's the moistest I've ever made or tasted.

MAKES 1 LOAF

- 11 tablespoons unsalted butter
- ½ cup packed light brown sugar
- 3 very ripe bananas, mashed
- ¼ cup dark rum
- ¼ cup Cognac
- 2 cups all-purpose flour
- 1 teaspoon table salt
- 1 teaspoon baking powder
- ½ teaspoon baking soda
- 1 cup sugar
- 2 large eggs, well beaten
- 1 tablespoon sour cream or buttermilk
- 1 cup chopped pecans or walnuts (optional)

FROM AUNT ELSA'S KITCHEN

Bananas can go from ripe to overripe very quickly. Peel and place them in a sturdy zip-top bag in the freezer until you can get around to making banana bread.

1. In a large skillet over medium heat, melt 3 tablespoons of the butter. Add the brown sugar and cook, stirring often, until the sugar melts completely and the mixture forms a smooth syrup, about 10 minutes. Reduce the heat if the sugar is browning too quickly. Don't worry if the sugar looks like it is clumping; it will smooth out as it cooks. Stir in the bananas, rum, and Cognac; the syrup will harden and become sticky. Cook 10 to 12 minutes, until the sugar has melted and the mixture is well blended. Remove from the heat and set aside to cool.

2. Preheat the oven to 350°F. Grease a 5 × 9-inch loaf pan and set aside.

3. In a large mixing bowl, place the flour, salt, baking powder, and baking soda. Whisk until well blended and set aside.

4. In the work bowl of an electric stand mixer fitted with the paddle attachment, or a large mixing bowl with a handheld mixer, place the sugar and remaining 8 tablespoons of butter. Beat on medium-high speed until fluffy and lightened in color, about 3 minutes. Add the eggs and beat until well blended.

5. Add the flour mixture and beat on medium speed just until blended. Add the reserved cooled bananas and the sour cream and beat just until blended. Fold in the nuts, if using. Pour into the prepared loaf pan. Bake until well browned and a toothpick inserted in the center comes out with just a few crumbs clinging to it, about 1 hour and 15 minutes. Transfer the pan to a cooling rack and let cool in the pan for 5 minutes. Unmold and let cool completely.

pumpkin bread

We always understood where our food came from. More often than not, the source was the land outside our back door! Pumpkin bread began with the pumpkin seed that we planted, tended, and eventually harvested. My mom never bought cans of cooked pumpkin, so the only time we could have pumpkin bread was when there was a surplus of pumpkins in our garden. This made me keenly aware of why pumpkins and pumpkin treats are a tradition for the autumn holidays—this is when pumpkins are actually in season! In fact, pumpkin bread is a Halloween tradition in my house. Those jack-o'-lanterns offer more than just spooky light—the pumpkins give us the makings for baking as well. I love cinnamon and this bread is definitely cinnamony, though you can use less if desired. As the bread bakes, the kitchen fills with a sweet, caramel aroma. The bread is very dark outside and very moist within.

MAKES 2 LOAVES

FOR THE PUMPKIN PUREE (SEE NOTE)

2½ cups chopped fresh pumpkin

½ cup packed light brown sugar

2 teaspoons ground cinnamon

NOTE
Alternatively, use 1 15-ounce can pumpkin pie filling.

FOR THE BREAD

3½ cups all-purpose flour

3 cups sugar

2 teaspoons baking soda

1 teaspoon table salt

2 tablespoons ground cinnamon

1 cup vegetable oil

4 large eggs, lightly beaten

1 cup coarsely chopped pecans

1. To prepare the pumpkin puree, place the pumpkin, sugar, and cinnamon in a medium saucepan. Add ¾ cup water and bring to a boil. Simmer, covered, for about 10 minutes, or until the pumpkin is very soft. Remove the pan from the heat and let stand until the pumpkin is completely cool. Drain off any excess water. Transfer the mixture to the work bowl of a food processor or blender and process until pureed. Set aside.

2. Preheat the oven to 350°F. Grease two 9 × 5-inch loaf pans.

3. In a large bowl, place the flour, sugar, baking soda, salt, and cinnamon. Whisk together until well blended.

4. In another large bowl, place the reserved pumpkin puree or the pumpkin pie filling, vegetable oil, eggs, and ½ cup water. Whisk until well blended.

5. Add the liquid ingredients to the dry ingredients and combine with a few strokes. Fold in the pecans. Transfer to the prepared pans and bake until well browned and a toothpick inserted in the center comes out clean, about 1 hour and 15 minutes.

6. Let the pans stand on cooling racks for 10 minutes. Unmold the breads and cool completely on the racks.

corn bread

In Texas it is a given that everybody needs a good recipe for corn bread, and here is mine. I like it warm from the oven slathered in butter. It's also good served with Chili con Carne (page 110).

(page 110).

MAKES 8 SERVINGS

1 cup cornmeal

1 cup all-purpose flour

2 teaspoons baking powder

½ teaspoon table salt

½ cup sugar

½ cup shortening, plus more for the pan

2 large eggs

1 cup milk

1 jalapeño, minced fine (optional)

Butter for serving (optional)

1. Preheat the oven to 400°F. Grease an 8-inch square pan and set aside.

2. In a medium mixing bowl, place the cornmeal, flour, baking powder, and salt. Whisk together until well blended.

3. In the work bowl of an electric stand mixer fitted with the paddle attachment, or in a large mixing bowl with a handheld mixer, place the sugar and shortening and beat on medium speed until well blended, 2 to 3 minutes, scraping down the sides of the bowl occasionally.

4. Add the eggs and beat until well combined, scraping down the side of the bowl. Add the milk and beat until blended. Add the cornmeal mixture and stir to combine. Stir in the jalapeños if desired.

5. Pour into the prepared pan and bake until the edges begin to pull away from the sides and a toothpick inserted in the middle comes out clean, about 30 minutes. Let cool in the pan for 10 minutes before slicing into squares and serving, preferably slathered with lots of butter!

desserts

From elegant fruit desserts and layer cakes filled and frosted with as many inches of frosting as they can hold to homey cookies and brownies, this chapter is all about celebrations big and small.

There are the Pan de Polvo cookies (page 188) that I have eaten at more *quinceañeras* and weddings than I can count. In my family, some part of the celebration always takes place in the kitchen, whether it's kids putting the final touch on Double Chocolate Chunk Cookies (page 192) or the No-Bake Peanut Balls (page 185) that are fun and easy for everyone to make. Chewy Brownies (page 196), Aunt Elsa's Pineapple Upside-Down Cake (page 211), and Beso's Churros (page 186) are so easy to prepare that they can be whipped up in a flash to mark any happy occasion, even the unexpected ones.

On these pages are several recipes that can be prepared in whole or in part long before your guests arrive, so you can enjoy the party and let your last course make a grand entrance without breaking a sweat. The components of the exuberant Chocolate Sweetheart Pie (page 197) can be prepared in advance and then composed in minutes. Elegant Individual Chocolate Cakes (page 203), bright and tangy Balsamic Strawberries (page 194), and beautiful Cranberry-Poached Pears (page 191) require only serving.

There are even baked desserts that celebrate the bounty of a season. The Strawberry Rhubarb Pie (page 198) is best made at the start of summer, when strawberries are in their prime. Many may consider carrot cake a year-round treat, but for me, Mom's Carrot Cake (page 204) always came from an abundant crop of carrots in our garden.

---

no-bake peanut balls

beso's churros

pan de polvo

cranberry-poached pears

double chocolate chunk cookies

balsamic strawberries

brownies

chocolate sweetheart pie

strawberry rhubarb pie

red velvet cake

individual chocolate cakes

mom's carrot cake

apple-spice layer cake with orange buttercream

aunt elsa's devil's food cake

aunt elsa's pineapple upside-down cake

no-bake peanut balls

The origins of this recipe are still a matter of open and often heated debate among my sisters and me, but there is one thing on which we can all agree: It is a favorite of my sister Elizabeth who has special needs. This recipe allows her to come into the kitchen with the rest of us and make something truly delicious. Salted peanuts are best; either cocktail or dry-roasted works well.

MAKES ABOUT 3 DOZEN

- 1 cup smooth or chunky peanut butter (not natural)
- ½ cup honey
- ½ cup powdered sugar
- 2 cups finely crushed salted peanuts

Special equipment: 3 dozen small paper candy cups

1. In a medium mixing bowl, place the peanut butter, honey, and powdered sugar. Stir until well blended and smooth.

2. Place the crushed peanuts in a shallow dish. Wet your hands and shake off the excess water. Scoop out a heaping teaspoon of the peanut butter mixture and roll it into a 1-inch ball. Place the ball in the crushed peanuts and gently roll until coated. Place the ball in a candy cup and continue with the remaining peanut mixture and peanuts. When all the balls are formed, refrigerate them until firm, about 1 hour. Serve.

3. Store in a tightly covered container in the refrigerator for up to 2 weeks.

FROM AUNT ELSA'S KITCHEN
When hand-rolling sticky doughs like this one, rinsing your hands in cool running water helps keep the mixture from sticking to them. Rinse several times as you work, and shake off the excess water each time.

EVA'S HEROES
My sister Elizabeth, who was born with a mental disability, is the oldest of my mom and dad's four daughters, so when my other two sisters and I came along, we were truly born into Liza's world. I am not exaggerating when I say Liza is my hero. Because of her, I co-founded Eva's Heroes, an organization based in San Antonio, Texas, that is dedicated to enriching the lives of those with developmental challenges by providing an inclusive setting so they can integrate and flourish in society. Eva's Heroes offers unique opportunities for these young men and women to experience what they may not be able to do elsewhere.

beso's churros

Churros are basically Mexican doughnuts: a lighter, fluffier version of the fried dough served at county fairs all over the country. We serve this to great acclaim at the Beso restaurants and they are heavenly eaten warm.

MAKES ABOUT 20

⅓ cup unsalted butter

Pinch of table salt

1 cup all-purpose flour

3 large eggs

½ cup sugar, for rolling the churros

1 tablespoon ground cinnamon, for rolling the churros

Vegetable oil, for frying

1. In a medium saucepan, place the butter, 1 cup of water, and salt. Bring to a boil over medium heat. Add the flour and stir over the heat until the mixture pulls away from the sides of the pot and comes together to form a cohesive dough, 30 seconds to 1 minute.

2. Transfer the flour mixture to the work bowl of an electric stand mixer fitted with the paddle attachment. Beating on low speed, add the eggs 1 at a time, and then continue to beat until they are thoroughly blended, about 2 minutes.

3. Fit a piping bag with a large star (number 7) tip. Place it in a tall drinking glass tip-end down and open the bag. Transfer the batter to the bag, filling it no more than halfway. Twist the top to push the batter down and into the tip. Set aside.

4. In a shallow bowl, place the sugar and cinnamon and stir with a fork until well blended. Set aside.

5. Line a baking sheet with paper towels. Pour the oil into a large skillet to 1 inch deep. Heat the oil over medium heat to 350°F.

6. Pipe 4-inch lengths of the dough directly into the hot oil. To release the dough from the piping bag, scrape the tip against the side of the pan or use a butter knife. Fry 3 or 4 pieces of dough at a time, turning once, until golden brown, about 4 minutes total. Adjust the heat as necessary to keep the oil temperature at 350°F. Use tongs to transfer the churros to the paper towels to drain. As soon as they are cool enough to handle, roll them in the cinnamon-sugar mixture until well coated. Serve warm.

pan de polvo

One year when I was very young I wanted to give pan de polvo, also called Mexican wedding cookies, as Christmas presents to my teachers at school. My mom taught me "her" recipe. In fact, it was this one—Aunt Elsa's!

I went to the flea market and spent my allowance on a collection of cookie cutters. I returned home and set out to make about 15 dozen in different shapes. Unfortunately, many of them broke because, as I discovered to my great frustration, pan de polvo is a very delicate cookie that doesn't hold shapes well—especially intricate ones like snowflakes. Those cookie cutters were probably my first purchase of kitchen equipment—but far from my last. They were so cheap that when I washed them for the first time, they rusted the next day!

Polvo means "powder," an apt description of a delicate cookie, generously rolled in sugar, that shatters on your tongue. I roll these very thin, just like Aunt Elsa used to, so they practically melt in your mouth. They are often rolled a little thicker, to about $^3/_8$ inch—if you do so, just bake them a little longer.

**MAKES ABOUT
8 DOZEN**

2½ cups all-purpose flour

1 teaspoon ground cinnamon

1 cup shortening

¼ cup sugar

**FOR THE SUGAR
COATING**

1 cup sugar

2 tablespoons ground cinnamon

1. In a medium mixing bowl, place the flour and cinnamon. Whisk together until thoroughly blended. Set aside.

2. In the work bowl of an electric stand mixer fitted with the paddle attachment, or in a large mixing bowl with a handheld mixer, beat the shortening and sugar on medium-high speed until well blended and fluffy, about 2 minutes. Add 2 tablespoons of water and beat until thoroughly combined.

3. Add the flour mixture and blend on medium-low just until completely blended. Press the dough into 2 equal disks. Place each disk between 2 sheets of wax paper. Use a rolling pin to roll out each disk to ⅛ inch thick, lifting and smoothing the top sheet of wax paper if necessary. Slide the two sheets of rolled dough onto a baking sheet. Chill until firm, about 30 minutes in the refrigerator or 10 minutes in the freezer.

4. Preheat the oven to 300°F.

5. Place one rolled dough on the work surface. Lift off and replace the top sheet of wax paper. Flip the dough over and lift off and set aside

the sheet of wax paper. Use a 1½-inch or smaller cookie cutter to cut into desired shapes. Transfer the cookies to an ungreased baking sheet, placing about 1 inch apart. Gather the scraps, reroll them between the sheets of wax paper, and refrigerate until firm. Repeat with the other sheet of dough.

6. Bake until firm when gently touched, 10 to 12 minutes. Let cool 3 minutes on the cookie sheet. Use a thin spatula to transfer them to cooling racks to cool completely.

7. To prepare the sugar coating, place the sugar and cinnamon in a shallow dish. Stir with a fork until completely combined. Roll the cooled cookies in the sugar and serve.

8. Store in a tightly covered container at room temperature for 3 to 4 days.

cranberry-poached pears

As they simmer, the pears send enticing wafts of fruit and vanilla through the air, a fitting invitation to a supremely elegant dessert. I've also served these at Thanksgiving with the main course in place of traditional cranberry sauce.

The tea bag adds undertones that complement or highlight the fruit in the simmering liquid—fruity or floral, depending on what you use. Choose a fruit tea that you like—I use tropical green tea or passion fruit.

MAKES 8 SERVINGS

- 8 small pears, such as Seckel, Forelle, or another variety, peeled, stems intact
- 5 tablespoons honey
- 3 tablespoons sugar
- 1 4- to 5-inch strip orange zest (removed with a vegetable peeler)
- 1 4- to 5-inch strip lemon zest (removed with a vegetable peeler)
- 1 teaspoon fresh lemon juice
- 1 3-inch cinnamon stick
- 1 vanilla bean, split lengthwise in half
- 1 fruit tea bag
- 2¾ cups (10 ounces) fresh or frozen cranberries

1. Place the pears in a saucepan large enough to hold them snugly. Add enough water (about 4 cups) to barely cover them. Add the honey, sugar, orange and lemon zests, lemon juice, and cinnamon stick.

2. Using the tip of a paring knife, scrape the vanilla seeds out of the pod and add them to the pan. Toss in the pod and add the tea bag. Bring to a boil over medium-high heat, stirring until the sugar has dissolved. Reduce the heat and simmer until the pears are tender when pierced with the tip of a knife, about 10 minutes.

3. Add the cranberries and return to a simmer until they burst, about 3 minutes. Remove and discard the tea bag.

4. Transfer the pears to a large bowl and pour over the cranberries and syrup. Cover and refrigerate overnight or up to 3 days.

5. Remove and discard the citrus zest, cinnamon stick, and vanilla bean. To serve, arrange the pears on a platter. Spoon over the cranberries and as much of the poaching liquid as desired. Serve.

double chocolate chunk cookies

With melted chocolate blended into the batter, chunks of chocolate throughout, and a shiny outer chocolate layer, these really should be called "triple" chocolate chunk cookies (see photograph, page 182). My nieces and I love to make these together. They do the very important—and fun!—job of dipping the cookies in the melted chocolate and arranging them carefully on wax paper to dry.

**MAKES ABOUT
15 COOKIES**

- 4 ounces good-quality semi-sweet chocolate, plus 4 ounces for dipping the cookies
- 1 cup all-purpose flour
- ½ teaspoon baking powder
- ¼ teaspoon table salt
- 8 tablespoons (1 stick) unsalted butter, at room temperature
- ½ cup granulated sugar
- ¼ cup firmly packed light brown sugar
- 1 large egg
- 1 teaspoon vanilla
- ¾ cup chopped walnuts (optional)

1. Place 1 ounce of the chocolate in a small dish and microwave on high power just until melted, 30 to 60 seconds, stopping and stirring every 10 to 15 seconds. Remove from the microwave, and stir until completely melted. Set aside.

2. Cut the remaining 3 ounces chocolate into ½-inch pieces. Set aside.

3. In a medium mixing bowl, place the flour, baking powder, and salt. Whisk together thoroughly and set aside.

4. In the work bowl of an electric mixer fitted with the paddle attachment, or in a large mixing bowl with a handheld mixer, place the butter, both sugars, egg, and vanilla. Beat on medium-high speed until light and fluffy, 2 to 3 minutes. Stir in the reserved melted chocolate. Add the flour mixture and beat on low just until thoroughly blended. Stir in the reserved chocolate chunks and the walnuts, if using. Refrigerate the dough for 30 minutes.

5. Preheat the oven to 375°F. Grease 2 cookie sheets.

6. Drop the dough by heaping tablespoonfuls onto the cookie sheets, spacing about 2 inches apart. Bake until lightly browned, 10 to 12 minutes, turning the sheets halfway through baking for even browning.

7. Let cool 5 minutes on the cookie sheets. Use a thin spatula to transfer them to cooling racks to cool completely.

8. Break or chop the remaining 4 ounces chocolate into ½-inch pieces and place them in a 1-cup glass measuring cup. Microwave on high just until melted, 1 to 2 minutes, stirring every 30 seconds. Remove from the microwave, and stir until completely melted.

9. Line cooling racks or baking sheets with wax paper. Dip each cooled cookie halfway in the melted chocolate and let the excess drip off. Place on the wax paper and let stand in a cool, dry place until the chocolate is firm. If the air is very humid, place in the refrigerator until the chocolate is set, about 30 minutes. Serve.

10. Store between layers of wax paper in a cool, dry place for up to 3 days.

balsamic strawberries

When I tell my guests that this is dessert, I often have to convince them that it really is acceptable to put vinegar on fresh berries. More than acceptable, actually, it is exquisite. Sweet-tart balsamic vinegar flavored with fruit is a perfect counterpoint to luscious, sweet strawberries. This is especially beautiful with large strawberries or with a combination of strawberries, raspberries, and blackberries.

MAKES 4 SERVINGS

- 1 16-ounce container ripe strawberries, hulled and quartered, or a combination of strawberries, raspberries, and blackberries (about 4 cups)
- ½ cup dark cherry- or raspberry-flavored balsamic vinegar
- Whipped cream

1. In a medium mixing bowl, place the berries and pour the vinegar over them. Place in the refrigerator for 30 minutes.

2. Use a slotted spoon to divide the berries among 4 champagne glasses—let as much or as little vinegar into the glass as desired. Top with a spoonful of whipped cream. Serve cold.

FROM AUNT ELSA'S KITCHEN
Use fresh strawberries in season—remember they are only truly in season locally for about 3 weeks, depending on where you live. Underripe berries are not sweet enough to offset the tart vinegar.

brownies

Brownie mixes are easy, I know, but what you gain in time you lose in flavor. This recipe comes together quickly and yields fudgy brownies with more chocolate taste than you'll ever get from a mix.

MAKES 20 BROWNIES

8 tablespoons (1 stick) unsalted butter

4 ounces bittersweet chocolate, coarsely chopped

3 large eggs

1½ cups sugar

1 teaspoon vanilla

1 cup all-purpose flour

¼ teaspoon table salt

1 cup chopped walnuts or pecans (optional)

1. Preheat the oven to 350°F. Grease a 9 × 12-inch baking pan.

2. In a heavy saucepan over very low heat, melt the butter and chocolate. Set aside to cool completely.

3. In a large mixing bowl, beat the eggs. Add the sugar and whisk until well blended. Add the cooled chocolate and the vanilla and stir until well blended. Add the flour, salt, and the nuts, if using, and stir just until combined.

4. Pour into the prepared pan and bake until a toothpick inserted into the center comes out with just a few crumbs clinging to it, about 25 minutes. Let the brownies stand in the pan on a wire rack until completely cool. Slice into squares and serve.

5. Store in a tightly covered container at room temperature for up to 4 days.

FROM AUNT ELSA'S KITCHEN
If using a glass baking dish, reduce the oven temperature to 325°F.

chocolate sweetheart pie

If ever a dessert earned the adage "more is more," this is it. Each and every time I serve this chocolate pie, piled high with chocolate-drizzled strawberries that hide a cloud of sweetened, vanilla-laced whipped cream, it elicits enthusiastic oohs and ahhs from my guests. They have no idea how incredibly easy it is to prepare.

MAKES 6 SERVINGS

- 1 store-bought, refrigerated, 9-inch piecrust
- 8 ounces semisweet (60%) chocolate
- 2/3 cup corn syrup
- 1 cup heavy cream
- 3 large eggs
- 2 tablespoons sugar
- 1/2 teaspoon vanilla
- 1 pint strawberries, hulled and sliced (about 2 cups)

1. Preheat the oven to 350°F. Line a 9-inch pie plate with the piecrust, gently pushing it into the edges of the pan. Place in the refrigerator until needed.

2. In a heavy saucepan, heat 6 ounces of the chocolate over low heat, stirring constantly, until just melted. Stir in the corn syrup and 1/2 cup of the cream. Add the eggs one at a time, beating well after each addition.

3. Place the pie shell on a baking sheet and pour the chocolate mixture into the pie shell. Bake until a knife inserted 1 inch from the center comes out clean, about 45 minutes. Let stand on a wire rack until completely cool; the center of the pie will sink as it cools.

4. In a medium mixing bowl, place the remaining 1/2 cup of cream, the sugar, and vanilla and beat until soft peaks form. Spoon the whipped cream onto the center of the cooled pie. Top with the strawberries.

5. Place the remaining 2 ounces of the chocolate in a small dish and microwave on high power just until melted, 30 to 60 seconds, stopping and stirring every 10 to 15 seconds. Remove from the microwave, and stir until completely melted. Drizzle the chocolate over the strawberries. Serve at room temperature.

strawberry rhubarb pie

Until I left Texas, I had never even heard of rhubarb, which grows in more temperate parts of the country. The first time I saw someone mix strawberries with rhubarb was when Cindy Crawford shared her recipe on *The Oprah Winfrey Show.* This odd-looking, sour-tasting fruit did not seem to me a good candidate for a pie so good that one would go on national television to sing its praises. But I decided I had to try it myself. I discovered a fruit filling with a beautiful shade of pink (lighter or darker, depending on the color of your rhubarb) and an invigorating tart-sweet flavor. At last I understand what all the fuss is about! Now as soon as rhubarb appears in markets, I begin to look for in-season strawberries so I can make this pie.

MAKES 6 TO 8 SERVINGS

- 16 ounces strawberries, hulled and quartered (about 4 cups)
- 1 pound rhubarb, cut into ½-inch pieces (about 4 cups)
- 1 cup sugar, plus about 2 teaspoons for sprinkling on top of pie
- ⅓ cup all-purpose flour
- 1 teaspoon vanilla extract
- Grated zest from 1 lemon
- Juice from 1 small lemon (2 tablespoons)
- 2 store-bought, refrigerated, 9-inch piecrusts
- 1 large egg white
- Whipped cream for serving

1. Position a rack in the center of the oven; preheat oven to 400°F.

2. In a large bowl, combine the strawberries, rhubarb, sugar, flour, vanilla, lemon zest, and lemon juice. Let stand for 10 minutes to allow the fruit to release its juices.

3. Meanwhile, line a 9-inch pie plate with one of the piecrusts, gently pushing it into the edges of the pan.

4. Use a slotted spoon to transfer the fruit into the piecrust.

5. Lay the second dough on a work surface. Using a pastry wheel, sharp knife, or a pizza wheel, cut the dough into ¾-inch-wide strips. Arrange half of the strips across the top of the pie, spacing them about ½ inch apart. Arrange the remaining strips across the top in the other direction, forming a lattice pattern. Fold the edges of the bottom crust up and over the ends of the strips.

6. To flute the edges: Hold the thumb and forefinger of one hand against the outer edge and use the forefinger of your other hand to gently push the other side of the dough into the small gap between your finger and thumb. Repeat around the entire edge of the pie.

7. In a small bowl, beat the egg white with 1 tablespoon of water. Brush the lattice strips lightly with the egg white wash and sprinkle with 1 to 2 teaspoons of sugar. Place the pie on a baking sheet.

8. Bake for 10 minutes, then reduce the oven temperature to 350°F. Bake until the pie is golden brown and the filling is bubbling in spots, about 55 minutes. Transfer to a cooling rack to cool. Serve with whipped cream.

red velvet cake

If you've ever seen the fabulous movie *Steel Magnolias,* you'll remember the running gag of a groom's cake in the shape of a giant armadillo that "looks like it's bleeding to death"! Until I saw that movie, I had no idea I could produce my favorite color in a cake. I left the theater determined to uncover the secret—which is, of course, red velvet cake. It's a deep red cake with velvety texture and a subtle flavor of cocoa hidden under snow white, vanilla-laced, cream cheese frosting. The armadillo shape is optional.

MAKES 8 TO 10 SERVINGS

FOR THE CAKE

- 4 teaspoons cocoa powder
- 2 ounces red food coloring
- 2 cups cake flour
- 1 teaspoon table salt
- 2 teaspoons baking soda
- 2 teaspoons distilled vinegar
- 1 cup shortening, at room temperature
- 1 cup sugar
- 2 large eggs
- 1 cup buttermilk
- 2 teaspoons vanilla
- Cream Cheese Frosting (recipe follows)

1. Position a rack in the center of the oven and preheat the oven to 350°F. Grease two 8-inch cake pans and line the bottoms with wax or parchment paper.

2. In a small bowl, place the cocoa powder and food coloring. Stir to combine and set aside.

3. In a medium bowl, sift together the flour and salt. Set aside.

4. In a small cup, place the baking soda and vinegar. Stir to combine and set aside.

5. In the work bowl of an electric stand mixer fitted with the paddle attachment, or in a large mixing bowl with a handheld mixer, place the shortening, sugar, and eggs. Beat on medium-high speed until well blended, 2 to 3 minutes, scraping down the sides of the bowl once or twice. Add the cocoa mixture and beat on medium just until combined. Add the flour mixture in 3 parts alternately with the buttermilk in 2 parts, starting and ending with the flour. Add the vanilla and beat on medium speed just until combined. Add the baking soda and vinegar mixture to the bowl. Use a rubber spatula to fold it into the batter, gently scraping down the sides of the bowl to make sure the batter is blended.

6. Pour the batter into the pans. Bake until the cake pulls away from the sides of the pan and springs back when lightly pressed in the middle, about 30 minutes.

(recipe continues)

7. Cool the cakes in the pans on a rack for 10 minutes. Run a thin knife around the outside and turn out onto racks. Peel off the paper. Flip them over to completely cool right-side up on the racks. If not assembling right away, cover the layers in plastic wrap and store at room temperature for 1 day.

8. When ready to fill and frost the cake, hold a serrated knife horizontally and use a gentle sawing motion to shave the domed top off each layer. Fill and frost the cake with cream cheese frosting, using a crumb coat (see box) if you have time.

9. Store in a tightly covered container at room temperature for up to 2 days.

FROM AUNT ELSA'S KITCHEN

If you have time after all the layers are filled, applying a "crumb coat" to the sides and top of a cake ensures that no crumbs get mixed into the frosting and mar the cake's appearance. To apply a crumb coat, place a small amount of the frosting in a dish and use an offset spatula to spread a thin coat all over the sides and top of the cake. Place in the refrigerator until firm, 20 to 30 minutes. Remove the cake from the refrigerator and frost the sides and top.

cream cheese frosting

I can't—don't want to!—imagine Red Velvet Cake (page 201) or Mom's Carrot Cake (page 204) without this luscious cream cheese frosting. This recipe makes a generous amount because, as far as I'm concerned, you can never have enough. So feel free to pile it between the layers and all over these or any other cakes (and to steal a spoonful or two just to taste along the way!).

MAKES 5½ CUPS

- 16 ounces cream cheese, at room temperature
- ½ pound (2 sticks) unsalted butter, at room temperature
- 1 pound powdered sugar, sifted
- 2 to 3 teaspoons vanilla (optional)

In the work bowl of an electric stand mixer fitted with the paddle attachment, or in a large mixing bowl with a handheld mixer, beat together the cream cheese and butter until fluffy. Add the sugar 1 cup at a time, blending between each addition. Mix in the vanilla, if using, and beat until very smooth, 3 to 5 minutes. Use at once or store in a tightly covered container in the refrigerator for up 3 days. Let stand at room temperature until soft and spreadable before using.

individual chocolate cakes

These individual molten chocolate cakes come from my ArtBites "Dining in the Aztec Empire" class, where I learned that chocolate is indigenous to Mexico, and for centuries nobles and priests used it to make an unsweetened drink.

MAKES 6 SERVINGS

6 tablespoons unsalted butter, plus about 2 tablespoons, melted, for the cake molds

4 tablespoons sugar, plus more for the cake molds

12 ounces bittersweet chocolate, coarsely chopped

4 large egg yolks

2 large egg whites

6 small sprigs of fresh mint, for garnish

Vanilla ice cream, for serving

1. Preheat the oven to 400°F. Brush six 4-ounce ramekins with the melted butter. Sprinkle the inside of each ramekin with sugar and tap out the excess. Place the ramekins on a rimmed baking sheet and refrigerate until needed.

2. In the top of a double boiler or a stainless-steel mixing bowl set over a pan of simmering water so that the bottom of the bowl does not touch the water, place 6 tablespoons of butter and the chocolate. Heat until melted and smooth. Set aside to cool slightly.

3. In a large mixing bowl, place 2 tablespoons of sugar and the egg yolks. Whisk until thoroughly blended. Add the chocolate mixture to the egg yolks and stir until well blended.

4. In the work bowl of an electric stand mixer fitted with the whisk attachment, or in a large mixing bowl with a handheld mixer, beat the egg whites on medium speed until they are frothy. Increase the speed gradually and beat until soft peaks form when the whisk is lifted out of the bowl. Sprinkle over the remaining 2 tablespoons of sugar and beat until the meringue is shiny and forms stiff peaks.

5. Fold about ¼ of the egg whites into the chocolate mixture and then gently fold the remaining egg whites into the chocolate mixture. Do not overmix; it is fine if there are a few streaks of egg white in the batter.

6. Pour the batter into the prepared ramekins. Bake until the cakes rise and then crack on top, and are gooey inside, 10 to 12 minutes.

7. Let cool slightly, then unmold onto individual plates. Garnish with mint and serve warm with vanilla ice cream.

mom's carrot cake

The carrots we grew were so sweet and delicious that we'd often go out to the garden, pull them one by one out of the ground, and bite right into them, with nothing more than a cursory wipe on our jeans on their journey from ground to mouth. An abundant crop would mean Mom would bake this divinely moist cake, which gave us the best reason ever to pray for a good harvest.

MAKES 8 TO 10 SERVINGS

2 cups all-purpose flour

1 tablespoon ground cinnamon

2 teaspoons baking powder

1 teaspoon baking soda

1 teaspoon table salt

1½ cups vegetable oil

2 cups sugar

4 large eggs, lightly beaten

3 cups peeled and coarsely grated carrots (from about 6 medium carrots)

Cream Cheese Frosting (page 202)

1 cup chopped pecans, for garnish

1. Preheat the oven to 350°F. Grease and flour two 8-inch cake pans.

2. Into a medium mixing bowl, sift together the flour, cinnamon, baking powder, baking soda, and salt three times. Set aside.

3. In the work bowl of an electric stand mixer fitted with the paddle attachment, or in a large mixing bowl with a handheld mixer, beat the oil and sugar until well blended. Add the eggs and beat until well combined. Add the flour mixture and stir just until blended. Add the carrots gradually, in small amounts, folding gently after each addition.

4. Pour into the prepared pans and bake until the cakes are lightly browned on top or a toothpick inserted in the center comes out clean, about 45 minutes.

5. Let the cake layers cool in the pans on wire racks for 5 minutes. Run a thin knife around the outside and turn out onto racks. Flip them over to completely cool right-side up on the racks. If not assembling right away, cover the layers in plastic wrap and store at room temperature for 1 day.

6. When ready to fill and frost the cake, hold a serrated knife horizontally and use a gentle sawing motion to shave the domed top off each layer. Fill and frost the cake with cream cheese frosting, using a crumb coat (page 202) if you have time. Top with pecans.

7. Store in a tightly covered container at room temperature for up to 2 days.

apple-spice layer cake with orange buttercream

I found this recipe in one of my aunt's cookbooks that is old enough to have seemed old when my aunt herself was a child. It's a great way to celebrate any event in autumn—or to celebrate autumn itself! Layers of spice-infused, walnut-studded apple cake hide an orange-flavored cream cheese filling and are covered with silky orange buttercream.

MAKES 8 TO 10 SERVINGS

FOR THE CAKE

2½ cups all-purpose flour

1½ teaspoons pumpkin pie spice

1 teaspoon baking powder

1 teaspoon baking soda

1 teaspoon table salt

8 tablespoons (1 stick) unsalted butter, at room temperature

1¾ cups sugar

3 large eggs

2 cups peeled, cored, and grated apples (from about 2 large apples)

1 teaspoon vanilla

½ cup milk

1 cup chopped walnuts

1. Preheat the oven to 350°F. Grease the bottom of three 8-inch cake pans. Line the pans with wax or parchment paper and grease the paper.

2. Into a large bowl, sift together the flour, pumpkin pie spice, baking powder, baking soda, and salt. Set aside.

3. In the work bowl of a food processor fitted with the paddle attachment, or in a large mixing bowl with a handheld mixer, beat together the butter and sugar until fluffy. Beat in the eggs one at a time, and beat until fluffy. Stir in the apples and vanilla.

4. Add the flour mixture in 3 parts alternately with the milk in 2 parts, starting and ending with the flour, and stirring just until blended after each addition. Fold in the walnuts.

5. Pour into the prepared pans. Bake until the center springs back when lightly pressed with a fingertip, about 35 minutes. Let the cake layers cool in the pans on wire racks for 5 minutes. Run a thin knife around the outside and turn out onto racks. Peel off the paper. Flip them over to completely cool right-side up on the racks. If not assembling right away, cover the layers in plastic wrap and store at room temperature for 1 day.

8 tablespoons (1 stick) unsalted butter, at room temperature

1½ pounds confectioners' sugar, sifted

¼ cup fresh orange juice

4 teaspoons grated orange rind

1 teaspoon vanilla

Pinch of table salt

1 8-ounce package cream cheese, at room temperature

FOR THE GARNISH
(optional)

1 cup walnut halves

1 apple, thinly sliced

Juice of 1 lemon

6. Meanwhile, prepare the orange buttercream frosting: In the work bowl of an electric stand mixer fitted with the paddle attachment, or in a large mixing bowl with a handheld mixer, beat the butter until soft. Add the sugar in 3 parts alternately with the orange juice in 2 parts, beating constantly until creamy and smooth. Stir in 3 teaspoons of the orange rind, along with the vanilla and salt. Set aside.

7. To prepare the filling, in a small bowl, mix the cream cheese with a fork until softened. Add ½ cup of the orange mixture and the remaining 1 teaspoon of orange zest and stir until well blended.

8. When ready to fill and frost the cake, hold a serrated knife horizontally and use a gentle sawing motion to shave the domed top off each layer. Arrange one layer on a cake serving plate. Place half of the filling on top and use an offset spatula to spread the filling to the edges of the layer. Place a second layer on top. Place the remaining filling on top and spread it as for the first layer. Top with the final cake layer.

9. Frost the sides and top of the cake with the frosting, using a crumb coat (page 202).

10. If desired, garnish the cake with nuts and apples: Decorate the sides of the cake with the nuts. In a small bowl, gently toss the apple slices in lemon juice and arrange them on top of the cake just before serving.

11. Store in a tightly covered container at room temperature for up to 2 days.

aunt elsa's devil's food cake

This is everything you want a chocolate cake to be. A simply prepared batter bakes up into a delicious cake with layers that have a tender crumb and good chocolate flavor. The frosting is beaten into billowy clouds of shiny chocolate goodness that spreads like silk.

MAKES 8 TO 10 SERVINGS; FROSTING MAKES 4½ TO 5 CUPS

FOR THE CAKE

- 3 ounces unsweetened chocolate, chopped
- 2½ cups cake flour, plus more for the pans
- 2 teaspoons baking soda
- ½ teaspoon table salt
- 8 tablespoons (1 stick) unsalted butter, at room temperature
- 2½ cups lightly packed light brown sugar
- 3 large eggs
- 2 teaspoons vanilla
- ½ cup buttermilk
- 1 cup boiling water

FOR THE FROSTING

- 4 ounces unsweetened chocolate, chopped
- 4 cups (1 pound) confectioners' sugar, sifted
- ½ cup hot water
- 1 large egg
- 8 tablespoons (1 stick) unsalted butter
- 1 teaspoon vanilla

1. In the top of a double boiler or in a stainless-steel mixing bowl set over a pan of simmering water so that the bottom of the bowl does not touch the water, melt the chocolate. Set aside to cool.

2. Preheat the oven to 350°F. Grease and flour three 8-inch cake pans.

3. In a large bowl, sift the flour with the baking soda and salt; set aside.

4. In the work bowl of an electric stand mixer fitted with the paddle attachment, or in a large mixing bowl with a handheld mixer, place the butter, brown sugar, eggs, and vanilla and beat on high speed until lightened in color, about 3 minutes, scraping down the sides occasionally.

5. Reduce the speed to low and beat in the chocolate. Add the flour mixture in 3 parts alternately with the buttermilk in 2 parts, starting and ending with the flour. Beat in the water until smooth.

6. Pour into the prepared pans. Bake until the cake pulls away from the sides and a toothpick inserted into the center comes out clean, 30 to 35 minutes.

7. Let the cake layers cool in the pans on wire racks for 5 minutes. Run a thin knife around the outside and turn out onto racks. Peel off the paper. Flip them over to completely cool right-side up on the racks. If not assembling right away, cover the layers in plastic wrap and store at room temperature for 1 day.

(recipe continues)

8. Meanwhile, prepare the frosting: In the top of a double boiler or in a stainless-steel mixing bowl set over a pan of simmering water so that the bottom of the bowl does not touch the water, melt the chocolate. Set aside to cool.

9. In the work bowl of an electric stand mixer fitted with the paddle attachment, or in a large mixing bowl with a handheld mixer, place the cooled, melted chocolate, the sugar, and the hot water. Beat on medium speed until smooth. Add the egg, butter, and vanilla. Continue beating until the frosting is thick and fluffy and mounds beautifully on a spoon, 2 to 3 minutes.

10. When ready to fill and frost the cake, hold a serrated knife horizontally and use a gentle sawing motion to shave the domed top off each layer. Fill and frost the cake, using a crumb coat (page 202) if you have time.

11. Store in a tightly covered container in the refrigerator for up to 2 days; let stand at room temperature for 30 minutes before serving.

FROM AUNT ELSA'S KITCHEN
If the percentages you sometimes see on bars of chocolate seem baffling, just know this: They refer to the percentage of cocoa solids and cocoa butter in the chocolate. This varies from brand to brand, but generally semisweet chocolate is about 50 percent cocoa, and bittersweet is 60 to 70 percent cocoa. Always use a good-quality chocolate in chocolate desserts—it will usually determine how good your end result is!

aunt elsa's pineapple upside-down cake

Buttery, not overly sweet, yellow cake is topped with rich, caramelized pineapple in this classic treat that never lets me down. All of the ingredients, including the pineapple, are staples in my pantry, so I can make it any time I want a cheerful and delicious dessert without having to shop especially for it. Using cake flour results in a more tender cake that is best eaten the day it is made. All-purpose flour gives a sturdier cake, almost like a coffee cake.

MAKES 8 SERVINGS

- ⅔ cup unsalted butter, at room temperature
- ½ cup packed light brown sugar
- 7 slices pineapple
- 7 drained maraschino cherries, or as needed (optional)
- 1½ cups cake flour or all-purpose flour
- 1 cup sugar
- 2 teaspoons baking powder
- ½ teaspoon table salt
- ⅔ cup milk
- 1 teaspoon vanilla
- 1 large egg

1. Preheat the oven to 350°F. In a flameproof 9-inch cake pan, melt ⅓ cup of the butter over low heat. Sprinkle the brown sugar evenly over the butter and cook, stirring, until the sugar and butter are blended and there are no pools of melted batter, 2 to 4 minutes.

2. Arrange the pineapple on top of the caramel. Decorate with cherries if desired, placing them in the center of each pineapple slice. Set the pan aside.

3. In the work bowl of an electric stand mixer fitted with the paddle attachment, or in a large mixing bowl with a handheld mixer, place the flour, sugar, baking powder, and salt and mix on low speed until well combined. Add the remaining ⅓ cup of butter along with the milk and vanilla. Beat on medium speed for 2 minutes. Scrape down the sides of the bowl. Add the egg and beat on medium speed for 2 minutes. Pour the batter over the pineapple.

4. Bake until the cake is golden brown and a toothpick inserted in the center comes out clean, 40 to 50 minutes. Remove the pan from the oven and carefully tilt it in all directions to release the cake from the sides of the pan. Let cool in the pan for about 3 minutes. Turn the pan over onto a serving plate and let stand for 2 to 3 minutes. Carefully lift the pan off the cake. Use a spatula to remove any fruit that is stuck to the pan and place it on the cake. Serve warm or at room temperature.

drinks

The drinks I prepare have a very important purpose: to quench the considerable thirst caused by the Texas heat. Many of these refreshing concoctions put to good use the fruit and herbs that grew around us when I was a kid: lemons, limes, mint, and strawberries. And while I love to drink wine with dinner, I don't otherwise drink much alcohol. My friends, on the other hand, adore cocktails, so many of my drink recipes can be adapted to include liquor. I gravitate to ice-cold, fruity, citrusy concoctions that are delicious with or without a shot of flavored rum or vodka. Even hot apple cider, which is my favorite drink around Christmas, is enhanced for some by a nice shot of rum. The rich smell of cinnamon and apples warms the spirit as much as sipping it warms the body.

limeade
strawberry daiquiri
mint lemonade
sweet sun tea
long island iced tea
hot apple cider

limeade

The limes we grew in Texas are almost a hybrid lemon-lime and we used them to make "ades." It wasn't until I was much older that I realized other people usually used lemons, not limes. This is the recipe I grew up with, and it works just as perfectly with the limes you can buy at the store as it did with the limes we grew.

MAKES ABOUT 7½ CUPS; 4 TO 6 SERVINGS

Juice from 8 limes (about 1 cup)

½ cup sugar or to taste

Ice, for serving

1. In a large pitcher, place 6 cups of room temperature water along with the lime juice and sugar. Stir until the sugar is dissolved, 1 to 2 minutes.

2. Place in the refrigerator and chill for 1 hour. Divide among 4 or 6 glasses and serve over ice.

strawberry daiquiri

We felt so fancy and elegant as children, sipping "virgin" strawberry daiquiris out of beautiful glasses. I still enjoy these without the rum, but when I do add it, I always choose a flavored rum for the delicious tropical fruit flavor it adds.

MAKES 3½ CUPS; 2 TO 3 SERVINGS

5 ounces frozen strawberries

½ banana

1 6-ounce can frozen lemonade

½ lemonade can (6 tablespoons; 3 ounces) of coconut, banana, or pineapple rum (optional)

2 tablespoons powdered sugar

About 12 (3½ cups) ice cubes or as needed

Up to ½ cup fresh orange juice, or to taste

1. In a blender, place the strawberries, banana, and frozen lemonade. Fill the empty lemonade can halfway with rum and add it to the blender with the sugar and ice. Blend until well combined and slushy. Add orange juice to thin the mixture if necessary or more ice cubes to make it thicker.

2. Divide among 2 or 3 glasses and serve.

mint lemonade

We had lemon trees and mint all over our ranch when I was a kid. I don't remember when I tasted the two together for the first time, but since then I've never liked lemonade any other way. For kids or anyone not drinking alcohol, it's a fabulously festive and beautiful nonalcoholic treat. Or add a shot of rum or vodka to each glass and make a cocktail out of it!

MAKES 3 CUPS; ABOUT 4 SERVINGS

FOR THE LEMONADE

½ cup sugar

¼ cup hot water

½ cup fresh lemon juice (from 4 lemons)

FOR MINT LEMONADE (2 SERVINGS)

About 12 (3½ cups) ice cubes

1½ cups lemonade, plus more if needed

6 to 7 sprigs of fresh mint, plus more for garnish

1. To prepare the lemonade, place the sugar and hot water in a 2-quart container. Close tightly and shake until the sugar is dissolved. Add the lemon juice and enough cold water to make 3 cups total. Shake until well combined.

2. To make 2 servings of mint lemonade, place the ice in a blender—it should fill the blender about halfway. Pour over the lemonade. Pull the leaves off the mint and add to the blender. Puree until well blended and slushy. If too liquidy, add more ice and puree; if too slushy, add a little more lemonade and puree until well blended.

3. Pour into two 12-ounce glasses. Garnish each with a mint sprig and serve immediately.

FROM AUNT ELSA'S KITCHEN
Citrus fruit such as limes, lemons, and oranges should always be stored at room temperature. Don't try to juice citrus that has been stored in the refrigerator; it does not release its juice as readily when it is cold.

sweet sun tea

In the South, we mean it when we offer you a tall glass of sweet tea—it is *sweet*! This is the real thing, infused with help from the hot sun and sweet enough to put a smile on anyone's face. Make sure to add the sugar right after you bring the warm tea in from the sun so it'll dissolve completely. Once the sweet tea is mixed, keep it refrigerated and discard it if it appears at all cloudy.

**MAKES 8 CUPS;
6 TO 8 SERVINGS**

- 8 bags black caffeinated tea
- 8 cups filtered water
- ¼ to ½ cup honey
- ¼ to ½ cup sugar
- 1 lemon, thinly sliced
- Ice, for serving

1. Wash a clear, glass pitcher in hot, soapy water and dry thoroughly. Place the tea bags in the pitcher and add the filtered water. Set in the full sun until the tea is nicely dark, 1 to 2 hours. Remove and discard the tea bags.

2. Add ¼ cup honey and ¼ cup sugar and stir until completely dissolved. Taste and continue to add honey and sugar until the tea reaches the desired sweetness.

3. Add the lemon slices to the tea and serve over ice. If not serving immediately, store in the refrigerator for 1 to 2 days.

FROM AUNT ELSA'S KITCHEN
Just float the lemon slices in the tea; don't squeeze the lemon juice into the full batch. The lemon juice alters the balance and acidity of the tea causing it to taste "off." Of course, once the sweet tea is served, folks can squeeze the lemon into their own glasses if they'd like.

long island iced tea

Traditionally, Long Island Iced Tea is made with clear liquors and a splash of cola to give it an iced tea color. Instead, my version depends on a fabulous vodka that my friend Virginia from Alabama gave me: sweet-tea-infused vodka from a small distillery called Firefly.

MAKES 2 SERVINGS

Ice

2 tablespoons silver tequila

2 tablespoons sweet-tea-infused vodka

2 tablespoons light rum

2 tablespoons triple sec

2 tablespoons gin

Juice from 3 small lemons (6 tablespoons)

2 teaspoons sugar

½ to ¾ cup cranberry juice

2 lemon wedges

1. Fill a shaker with ice, and pour in the tequila, sweet-tea-infused vodka, rum, triple sec, gin, lemon juice, and sugar. Shake for about 20 seconds, until the shaker is freezing cold on the outside. Fill 2 pint glasses about three-quarters with ice, then pour the cocktail mixture over the ice.

2. Top off with enough cranberry juice to make the drink the color of iced tea. Garnish each glass with a lemon wedge and serve.

hot apple cider

MAKES 8 CUPS; ABOUT 6 SERVINGS

½ gallon apple cider

2 3-inch cinnamon sticks, plus more for serving

6 whole cloves

6 whole allspice

1 teaspoon grated nutmeg

Cinnamon sticks, for garnish

This is a Christmas favorite at my house, perfect for everything from big holiday parties to a quiet winter night at home. Sometimes I put a batch of it on to simmer just because its delicious fragrance of warm spice and apple fills the house and makes me happy.

1. In a Crock-Pot place the apple cider, cinnamon sticks, cloves, allspice, and nutmeg. Heat over low heat until hot, about 30 minutes.

2. Serve hot in mugs; place a cinnamon stick in each mug as garnish.

resources

EATWILD

P.O. Box 7321
Tacoma, WA 98417
866-453-8489
www.eatwild.com

To find local farms with
pasture-fed meat.

ENVIRONMENTAL WORKING GROUP

1436 U Street NW, Suite 100
Washington, DC 20009
202-667-6982
www.ewg.org

To find out which are the most
and least pesticide-laden fruits
and vegetables.

EVA'S HEROES

11107 Wurzbach Road,
Suite 203
San Antonio, TX 78230
210-694-9090
www.evasheroes.org

A nonprofit organization dedicated to helping developmentally challenged children and
young adults between 14 and
21 years of age integrate and
flourish in society.

LOCALHARVEST

P.O. Box 1292
Santa Cruz, CA 95061
831-515-5602
www.localharvest.org

To locate local farmers' markets and grocery stores where
you can find sustainable and
organic produce, poultry,
meat, and eggs.

MONTEREY BAY AQUARIUM'S SEAFOOD WATCH PROGRAM

886 Cannery Row
Monterey, CA 93940
831-648-4888
www.seafoodwatch.org

For a regularly updated list
of which fish and shellfish
are "best choices" and "good
alternatives," and which you
should avoid.

acknowledgments

When I was approached by Jennifer Gates to do a cookbook, I was immediately inspired and excited. Then reality sunk in that I had never written down most of my recipes. They were all in my head, with a "pinch of this" and a "dash of that." Thanks to Jennifer, she placed me in the right hands at Clarkson Potter with Emily Takoudes, who patiently listened to my ideas and thoughts about food and cooking. Emily then paired me up with an angel named Marah Stets, who was responsible for breaking into my brain and prying out all of the recipes that were trapped in my mind for more than twenty years. Marah and I have created a special bond that I will cherish forever. Thank you, Marah, for your incomparable work ethic and your amazing talent as a writer; you brought to life this entire cookbook that was dormant in my head.

Once the book was constructed it was time to photograph the food, and we couldn't think of a better person to do this than Ben Fink. Thank you, Ben, for making my simple tacos look like a work of art. You are a genius at what you do. A very special thanks to Randall Slavin, who captured my spirit of cooking with my family and friends through some of the most beautiful photos in this book; your loving energy is seen in each of these photos. And I'm grateful to Potter's art director, Jane Treuhaft, for her great artistic eye that makes this book pop right off the shelf! Also thank you to Jennifer Davis for designing a beautiful book.

This book would not have been possible without my family, whose support and love have carried me through everything in life. Thank you to my mom for allowing me to discover cooking through the lens of being a Mexican American; if I can be a fraction of the woman you are, then I have succeeded. And thank you to my dad for teaching me how all food deserves respect and is best served in its most natural state. I also thank my three loving sisters, Liza, Emily, and Esmeralda, for letting me be the spoiled, rotten baby of the family; all three of you had such an influence on me and helped craft me into the woman I am today, and I love you. To my soul sisters, Bonnie, Brittany, Alina, Maria, Virginia, Sandra, Christiane, and Monica, thanks for being the guinea pigs for my cooking; my favorite memories include standing in my kitchen, cooking, drinking, and talking about life, so I thank you from the bottom of my heart for being my willing audience.

Finally, I give thanks to my greatest inspiration, Aunt Elsa, who taught the entire family everything about food and catering and how to make home anywhere you are in the world; I miss you every day.

index

Note: Page references in *italics* refer to photographs.

Aïoli, Chipotle, 162, *163*
Almonds
  Hot Chicken Salad, 79
Ants on a Log, 24, *24*
Appetizers
  Ants on a Log, 24, *24*
  Argentinean Empanadas, 38–39, *39*
  Avocado Stuffed with Shrimp, *28,* 29
  Cannellini Beans with Crushed Red Pepper, *22,* 23
  Ceviche, 30, *31*
  Chunky Guacamole with Serrano Peppers, *18,* 19
  Dad's Shrimp Cocktail, 26, *27*
  Goat Cheese Balls, *32,* 33
  Hot Artichoke Dip, 17
  Normandy Shrimp, 25
  Pico de Gallo, 20, *21*
  Sweet-Potato Empanadas, 36–37
  Tostones, 34, *35*
Apple Cider, Hot, 219
Apple-Spice Layer Cake with Orange Buttercream, 206–7
Argentinean Empanadas, 38–39, *39*
Artichoke(s)
  Dip, Hot, 17
  Hearts of Palm Salad, 57
  Hot Chicken Salad, 79
Arugula
  Grilled Shrimp on, 52, *53*
  Hearts of Palm Salad, 57
Asparagus
  Broiled, *144,* 145
  with Grey Moss Inn White French Dressing, 64, *65*
Aunt Didi's Carne Guisada, 107
Aunt Edna's Homemade Flour Tortillas, 171–73, *172*
Aunt Elsa's Buttermilk Biscuits, *176,* 177
Aunt Elsa's Devil's Food Cake, *208,* 209–10
Aunt Elsa's Pineapple Upside-Down Cake, 211
Avocado(s)
  Ceviche, 30, *31*
  Chalupas, *86,* 87
  choosing and preparing, 60
  Chunky Guacamole with Serrano Peppers, *18,* 19
  Dad's Shrimp Cocktail, 26, *27*
  Mexican Caprese, 60, *61*

Stuffed with Shrimp, *28,* 29
  Tortilla Soup, *44,* 45–46

Baked Goat Cheese Rigatoni, 131
Balsamic Reduction, Sweet, 165
Balsamic Strawberries, 194, *195*
Balsamic Vinaigrette, 159
Banana(s)
  Bread, 178, *179*
  overripe, freezing, 178
Basil-Tomato Spaghetti, *136,* 137
BBQ Chicken Pizza, *90,* 91
BBQ Sauce, 164
Beans
  Black, 127
  Borracho, 128–29, *129*
  Cannellini, with Crushed Red Pepper, *22,* 23
  Chalupas, *86,* 87
  Chili con Carne, 110
  dried, buying and cooking, 127
  Green, Garlic, *140,* 141
  Grilled Shrimp on Arugula, 52, *53*
  Refried, 130, *130*
Beef
  Argentinean Empanadas, 38–39, *39*
  Aunt Didi's Carne Guisada, 107
  Beer-Braised Brisket, 101
  Bolognese, 111
  Broth, 114
  Chicken Fried Steak with White Gravy, 106
  Chili con Carne, 110
  Chili-Rubbed Skirt Steak Tacos, 102, *103*
  Crock-Pot Cuban Ropa Vieja, *112,* 113
  Filets Mignons with Sweet Balsamic Reduction, 108, *109*
  Flank Steak with Lime Marinade, *104,* 105
  Meat Loaf, 115
  Mexican Lasagna, *118,* 119
  Stuffed Green Peppers, 116, *117*
Beer-Braised Brisket, 101
Beets
  cooking methods, 55
  and Goat Cheese, Baby Spinach with, 55
  peeling, 55
Berries
  Balsamic Strawberries, 194, *195*
  Butterhead Lettuce Salad with Strawberries, *58,* 59
  Chocolate Sweetheart Pie, 197
  Cranberry-Poached Pears, *190,* 191

Strawberry Daiquiri, 215
  Strawberry Rhubarb Pie, 198–99, *199*
Beso's Churros, 186, *187*
Biscuits, Buttermilk, Aunt Elsa's, *176,* 177
Black Beans, 127
Borracho Beans, 128–29, *129*
Brazilian Leeks, 142, *143*
Bread(s). *See also* Tortilla(s)
  Aunt Elsa's Buttermilk Biscuits, *176,* 177
  Banana, 178, *179*
  Corn, 181
  crumbs, panko, about, 80
  Pumpkin, 180
  Toast Triangles, 17
Broccoli and Rice Casserole, 123
Broiled Asparagus, *144,* 145
Broth
  Beef, 114
  Chicken, 51
  Vegetable, 49
Brownies, 196
Brussels Sprouts, Spicy Roasted, 138, *139*
Butter
  for recipes, 13
  Sauce, Lemon, 166
Buttercream Frosting, Orange, 207
Butterhead Lettuce Salad with Strawberries, *58,* 59
Buttermilk
  Biscuits, Aunt Elsa's, *176,* 177
  Dressing, 161
Butternut Squash
  Soup, 43
  storing, 43

Cakes
  Apple-Spice Layer, with Orange Buttercream, 206–7
  applying frosting to, tip for, 202
  Carrot, Mom's, 204
  Chocolate, Individual, 203
  Devil's Food, Aunt Elsa's, *208,* 209–10
  Pineapple Upside-Down, Aunt Elsa's, 211
  Red Velvet, *200,* 201–2
Cannellini Beans with Crushed Red Pepper, *22,* 23
Carne Guisada, Aunt Didi's, 107
Carrot
  Cake, Mom's, 204
  -Ginger Soup, 48, *49*
Catfish Fillets, Crispy and Spicy, 69
Celery
  Ants on a Log, 24, *24*
Ceviche, 30, *31*
Chalupas, *86,* 87
Cheese. *See also* Cream Cheese; Queso fresco

Argentinean Empanadas, 38–39, *39*
  BBQ Chicken Pizza, *90,* 91
  Butterhead Lettuce Salad with Strawberries, *58,* 59
  Chalupas, *86,* 87
  Eggplant Parmesan, 154–55
  Goat, and Beets, Baby Spinach with, 55
  Goat, Balls, *32,* 33
  Goat, Rigatoni, Baked, 131
  Hot Chicken Salad, 79
  Mexican Caprese, 60, *61*
  Mexican Lasagna, *118,* 119
Chicken
  BBQ, Pizza, *90,* 91
  Breasts, Boneless, Skinless, Roasted, 89
  Broth, 51
  with Caramelized Shallots and Shiitake-Wine Sauce, *82,* 83
  Chalupas, *86,* 87
  Enchiladas Rojas (Red Enchiladas), 94–96, *95*
  Flautas, *92,* 93
  Hungarian Paprika, 84, *85*
  Lemon Fried, 80, *81*
  Poached, 89
  Salad, Hot, 79
  Salad Sandwiches, 88
  Tortilla Soup, *44,* 45–46
Chicken Fried Steak with White Gravy, 106
Chiles
  Chili con Carne, 110
  Chipotle Aïoli, 162, *163*
  chipotles in adobo, storing, 162
  Chunky Guacamole with Serrano Peppers, *18,* 19
  Enchiladas Rojas (Red Enchiladas), 94–96, *95*
  Mexican Lasagna, *118,* 119
  Pico de Gallo, 20, *21*
  Tortilla Soup, *44,* 45–46
  varieties of, 20, 96
  Veracruz Corn, *150,* 151–52
Chili con Carne, 110
Chili-Rubbed Skirt Steak Tacos, 102, *103*
Chipotle Aïoli, 162, *163*
Chipotles in adobo, storing, 162
Chocolate
  Aunt Elsa's Devil's Food Cake, *208,* 209–10
  Brownies, 196
  Cakes, Individual, 203
  cocoa percentages in, 210
  Double, Chunk Cookies, *182,* 192–93
  Sweetheart Pie, 197
Chorizo
  Chili con Carne, 110
  Chunky Guacamole with Serrano Peppers, *18,* 19
Churros, Beso's, 186, *187*
Cider, Hot Apple, 219

Citrus. *See also* Lemon(s); Lime(s); Orange(s)
-Garlic Sauce, 165
juicing, 216
storing, 216
Cookies and bars
Brownies, 196
Double Chocolate Chunk Cookies, *182*, 192–93
Pan de Polvo, 188–89, *189*
Corn
removing silk from cob, 63
Veracruz, *150*, 151–52
and Zucchini Salad, *62*, 63
Corn Bread, 181
Corn Tortillas, 174, *175*
Crabmeat
Ceviche, 30, *31*
Cranberry-Poached Pears, *190*, 191
Cream Cheese
Frosting, 202
Orange Buttercream Frosting, 207
Crispy and Spicy Catfish Fillets, 69
Cuban Ropa Vieja, Crock-Pot, *112*, 113

Dad's Shrimp Cocktail, 26, *27*
Daiquiri, Strawberry, 215
Deep-frying, tips for, 37
Desserts
Apple-Spice Layer Cake with Orange Buttercream, 206–7
Aunt Elsa's Devil's Food Cake, *208*, 209–10
Aunt Elsa's Pineapple Upside-Down Cake, 211
Balsamic Strawberries, 194, *195*
Beso's Churros, 186, *187*
Brownies, 196
Chocolate Sweetheart Pie, 197
Cranberry-Poached Pears, *190*, 191
Double Chocolate Chunk Cookies, *182*, 192–93
Individual Chocolate Cakes, 203
Mom's Carrot Cake, 204
No-Bake Peanut Balls, 185
Pan de Polvo, 188–89, *189*
Red Velvet Cake, *200*, 201–2
Strawberry Rhubarb Pie, 198–99, *199*
Dips
Artichoke, Hot, 17
Cannellini Beans with Crushed Red Pepper, *22*, 23
Chunky Guacamole with Serrano Peppers, *18*, 19
Pico de Gallo, 20, *21*
Double Chocolate Chunk Cookies, *182*, 192–93

Dover Sole, Lemon, 70, *71*
Drinks
Hot Apple Cider, 219
Limeade, 215
Long Island Iced Tea, 219
Mint Lemonade, 216, *217*
Strawberry Daiquiri, 215
Sweet Sun Tea, 218

Eggplant Parmesan, 154–55
Eggs, organic, buying, 79
Empanadas
Argentinean, 38–39, *39*
Sweet-Potato, 36–37
Enchiladas Rojas (Red Enchiladas), 94–96, *95*

Filets Mignons with Sweet Balsamic Reduction, 108, *109*
Fish. *See also* Shellfish
Crispy and Spicy Catfish Fillets, 69
Herbed Sea Bass in Parchment, 75
Honey-Glazed Salmon, *72*, 73
Lemon Dover Sole, 70, *71*
Tilapia with Citrus-Garlic Sauce, 74, *74*
Flank Steak with Lime Marinade, *104*, 105
Flautas, *92*, 93
Fried Plantains, 153
Frostings
Cream Cheese, 202
Orange Buttercream, 207
spreading on cakes, tips for, 202
Fruits. *See also* Berries; *specific fruits*
citrus, juicing, 216

Garlic
-Citrus Sauce, 165
Green Beans, *140*, 141
Lemon Dressing, 159
Mashed Potatoes, 149
Ginger-Carrot Soup, 48, *49*
Goat Cheese
Balls, *32*, 33
and Beets, Baby Spinach with, 55
Rigatoni, Baked, 131
Grains. *See* Rice
Green Beans
Garlic, *140*, 141
Grilled Shrimp on Arugula, 52, *53*
Greens. *See also* Lettuce
Baby Spinach with Beets and Goat Cheese, 55
Grilled Shrimp on Arugula, 52, *53*
Hearts of Palm Salad, 57
Grey Moss Inn White French Dressing, 160
Grill Sauce, Steak, 164
Guacamole, Chunky, with Serrano Peppers, *18*, 19

Hearts of Palm Salad, 57
Herbs
fresh, storing, 161
Herbed Sea Bass in Parchment, 75
Mint Lemonade, 216, *217*
Tomato-Basil Spaghetti, *136*, 137
Honey-Glazed Salmon, *72*, 73
Hot Apple Cider, 219
Hot Artichoke Dip, 17
Hot Chicken Salad, 79
Hungarian Paprika Chicken, 84, *85*

Individual Chocolate Cakes, 203

Kimchi
Spicy Roasted Brussels Sprouts, 138, *139*

Lasagna, Mexican, *118*, 119
Leeks, Brazilian, 142, *143*
Lemon(s)
Butter Sauce, 166
Citrus-Garlic Sauce, 165
Dover Sole, 70, *71*
Fettuccine, 134, *135*
Fried Chicken, 80, *81*
Garlic Dressing, 159
juicing, 216
Mint Lemonade, 216, *217*
Orzo Soup, *50*, 51
for recipes, 13
storing, 216
Lettuce
Butterhead, Salad with Strawberries, *58*, 59
Chalupas, *86*, 87
Tortilla Soup, *44*, 45–46
Lime(s)
Citrus-Garlic Sauce, 165
juicing, 216
Limeade, 215
Marinade, Flank Steak with, *104*, 105
for recipes, 13
storing, 216
Long Island Iced Tea, 219

Main dishes
Aunt Didi's Carne Guisada, 107
BBQ Chicken Pizza, *90*, 91
Beef Bolognese, 111
Beer-Braised Brisket, 101
Chalupas, *86*, 87
Chicken Fried Steak with White Gravy, 106
Chicken Salad Sandwiches, 88
Chicken with Caramelized Shallots and Shiitake-Wine Sauce, *82*, 83
Chili con Carne, 110
Chili-Rubbed Skirt Steak Tacos, 102, *103*
Crispy and Spicy Catfish Fillets, 69

Crock-Pot Cuban Ropa Vieja, *112*, 113
Enchiladas Rojas (Red Enchiladas), 94–96, *95*
Filets Mignons with Sweet Balsamic Reduction, 108, *109*
Flank Steak with Lime Marinade, *104*, 105
Flautas, *92*, 93
Herbed Sea Bass in Parchment, 75
Honey-Glazed Salmon, *72*, 73
Hot Chicken Salad, 79
Hungarian Paprika Chicken, 84, *85*
Lemon Dover Sole, 70, *71*
Lemon Fried Chicken, 80, *81*
Meat Loaf, 115
Mexican Lasagna, *118*, 119
Stuffed Green Peppers, 116, *117*
Tilapia with Citrus-Garlic Sauce, 74, *74*
Turkey Shepherd's Pie, 97
Meat. *See* Beef; Chorizo
Meat Loaf, 115
Mexican Caprese, 60, *61*
Mexican Rice, 124, *125*
Mint Lemonade, 216, *217*
Mom's Carrot Cake, 204
Mushrooms
Chicken with Caramelized Shallots and Shiitake-Wine Sauce, *82*, 83
Portobello, 148, *148*
Shiitake-Wine Sauce, 167

No-Bake Peanut Balls, 185
Noodles
buying in bulk, 126
fideo, buying, 133
Hungarian Paprika Chicken, 84, *85*
Sopa de Fideo, *132*, 133
Normandy Shrimp, 25
Nuts
Apple-Spice Layer Cake with Orange Buttercream, 206–7
Butterhead Lettuce Salad with Strawberries, *58*, 59
Hot Chicken Salad, 79
Mom's Carrot Cake, 204
No-Bake Peanut Balls, 185
Pumpkin Bread, 180

Olives
Argentinean Empanadas, 38–39, *39*
Orange(s)
Buttercream Frosting, 207
juicing, 216
storing, 216

Pan de Polvo, 188–89, *189*
Panko bread crumbs, about, 80

Paprika Chicken, Hungarian, 84, *85*
Parmesan Summer Squash, 146, *147*
Pasta. *See also* Noodles
  Baked Goat Cheese Rigatoni, 131
  Lemon Fettuccine, 134, *135*
  Lemon Orzo Soup, *50,* 51
  Rotini, Salad, 56, *56*
  Sopa de Fideo, *132,* 133
  Tomato-Basil Spaghetti, *136,* 137
Peanut Balls, No-Bake, 185
Peanut butter
  Ants on a Log, 24, *24*
  No-Bake Peanut Balls, 185
Pears, Cranberry-Poached, *190,* 191
Pecans
  Chicken Salad Sandwiches, 88
  Mom's Carrot Cake, 204
  Pumpkin Bread, 180
Peppers. *See also* Chiles
  Crock-Pot Cuban Ropa Vieja, *112,* 113
  Green, Stuffed, 116, *117*
  Hungarian Paprika Chicken, 84, *85*
  Rotini Pasta Salad, 56, *56*
  varieties of, 20
Pico de Gallo, 20, *21*
Pies
  Chocolate Sweetheart, 197
  Strawberry Rhubarb, 198–99, *199*
Pineapple Upside-Down Cake, Aunt Elsa's, 211
Pizza, BBQ Chicken, *90,* 91
Plantains
  buying, 153
  Fried, 153
  ripening, 153
  Tostones, 34, *35*
Pork sausages. *See* Chorizo
Portobello Mushrooms, 148, *148*
Potato(es)
  Garlic Mashed, 149
  Sweet-, Empanadas, 36–37
  Turkey Shepherd's Pie, 97
Poultry. *See also* Chicken
  Mexican Lasagna, *118,* 119
  organic, buying, 79
  Turkey Shepherd's Pie, 97
Pumpkin Bread, 180

Queso fresco
  about, 152
  Chalupas, *86,* 87
  Enchiladas Rojas (Red Enchiladas), 94–96, *95*
  Flautas, *92,* 93
  Tortilla Soup, *44,* 45–46
  Veracruz Corn, *150,* 151–52

Raisins
  Ants on a Log, 24, *24*
Red Velvet Cake, *200,* 201–2
Refried Beans, 130, *130*

Rhubarb Strawberry Pie, 198–99, *199*
Rice
  and Broccoli Casserole, 123
  buying in bulk, 126
  Mexican, 124, *125*
  White, 126
Ropa Vieja, Crock-Pot Cuban, *112,* 113
Rotini Pasta Salad, 56, *56*

Salad dressings
  Balsamic Vinaigrette, 159
  Buttermilk Dressing, 161
  Grey Moss Inn White French Dressing, 160
  Lemon Garlic Dressing, 159
Salads
  Asparagus with Grey Moss Inn White French Dressing, 64, *65*
  Baby Spinach with Beets and Goat Cheese, 55
  Butterhead Lettuce, with Strawberries, *58,* 59
  Corn and Zucchini, *62,* 63
  Grilled Shrimp on Arugula, 52, *53*
  Hearts of Palm, 57
  Mexican Caprese, 60, *61*
  Rotini Pasta, 56, *56*
Salmon, Honey-Glazed, *72,* 73
Salt, for recipes, 13
Sandwiches, Chicken Salad, 88
Sauces
  BBQ, 164
  Beef Bolognese, 111
  Chipotle Aïoli, 162, *163*
  Citrus-Garlic, 165
  Lemon Butter, 166
  Shiitake-Wine, 167
  Steak Grill, 164
  Sweet Balsamic Reduction, 165
Sausages. *See* Chorizo
Sea Bass, Herbed, in Parchment, 75
Seafood. *See* Fish; Shellfish
Shallots, Caramelized, and Shiitake-Wine Sauce, Chicken with, *82,* 83
Shellfish
  Avocado Stuffed with Shrimp, *28,* 29
  Ceviche, 30, *31*
  Dad's Shrimp Cocktail, 26, *27*
  Grilled Shrimp on Arugula, 52, *53*
  Normandy Shrimp, 25
  shrimp cooking directions, 25
  shrimp sizes and counts, 25
Shepherd's Pie, Turkey, 97
Shiitake-Wine Sauce, 167
Shortening, for recipes, 13
Shrimp
  Avocado Stuffed with, *28,* 29
  Ceviche, 30, *31*

  Cocktail, Dad's, 26, *27*
  cooking directions, 25
  Grilled, on Arugula, 52, *53*
  Normandy, 25
  sizes and counts, 25
Sides
  Baked Goat Cheese Rigatoni, 131
  Black Beans, 127
  Borracho Beans, 128–29, *129*
  Brazilian Leeks, 142, *143*
  Broccoli and Rice Casserole, 123
  Broiled Asparagus, *144,* 145
  Eggplant Parmesan, 154–55
  Fried Plantains, 153
  Garlic Green Beans, *140,* 141
  Garlic Mashed Potatoes, 149
  Lemon Fettuccine, 134, *135*
  Mexican Rice, 124, *125*
  Parmesan Summer Squash, 146, *147*
  Portobello Mushrooms, 148, *148*
  Refried Beans, 130, *130*
  Sopa de Fideo, *132,* 133
  Spicy Roasted Brussels Sprouts, 138, *139*
  Tomato-Basil Spaghetti, *136,* 137
  Veracruz Corn, *150,* 151–52
  White Rice, 126
Sopa de Fideo, *132,* 133
Soups. *See also* Broth; Stews
  Butternut Squash, 43
  Carrot-Ginger, 48, *49*
  Lemon Orzo, *50,* 51
  Tortilla, *44,* 45–46
  Yellow Squash, with Lemon, 47
Spicy Roasted Brussels Sprouts, 138, *139*
Spinach, Baby, with Beets and Goat Cheese, 55
Squash
  Butternut, Soup, 43
  butternut, storing, 43
  Corn and Zucchini Salad, *62,* 63
  Pumpkin Bread, 180
  Summer, Parmesan, 146, *147*
  Yellow, Soup with Lemon, 47
Steak Grill Sauce, 164
Stews
  Aunt Didi's Carne Guisada, 107
  Chili con Carne, 110
  Hungarian Paprika Chicken, 84, *85*
Strawberry(ies)
  Balsamic, 194, *195*
  Butterhead Lettuce Salad with, *58,* 59
  Chocolate Sweetheart Pie, 197
  Daiquiri, 215
  Rhubarb Pie, 198–99, *199*

Stuffed Green Peppers, 116, *117*
Sweet Balsamic Reduction, 165
Sweet-Potato Empanadas, 36–37
Sweet Sun Tea, 218

Tacos, Chili-Rubbed Skirt Steak, 102, *103*
Tea, Sweet Sun, 218
Tilapia with Citrus-Garlic Sauce, 74, *74*
Toast Triangles, 17
Tomatillos
  Flautas, *92,* 93
Tomato(es)
  -Basil Spaghetti, *136,* 137
  Ceviche, 30, *31*
  Chunky Guacamole with Serrano Peppers, *18,* 19
  Enchiladas Rojas (Red Enchiladas), 94–96, *95*
  Grilled Shrimp on Arugula, 52, *53*
  Mexican Caprese, 60, *61*
  Pico de Gallo, 20, *21*
  Rotini Pasta Salad, 56, *56*
Tortilla(s)
  Chalupas, *86,* 87
  Chili-Rubbed Skirt Steak Tacos, 102, *103*
  Corn, 174, *175*
  Enchiladas Rojas (Red Enchiladas), 94–96, *95*
  essential equipment for, 173
  Flour, Aunt Edna's Homemade, 171–73, *172*
  Mexican Lasagna, *118,* 119
  Soup, *44,* 45–46
  Veracruz Corn, *150,* 151–52
Tostones, 34, *35*
Turkey
  Mexican Lasagna, *118,* 119
  Shepherd's Pie, 97

Vegetable(s). *See also* specific vegetables
  Broth, 49
  green, blanching and shocking, 141
  green, health benefits, 145
  Veracruz Corn, *150,* 151–52
  Vinaigrette, Balsamic, 159
Vinegar, for recipes, 13

Walnuts
  Apple-Spice Layer Cake with Orange Buttercream, 206–7
  Butterhead Lettuce Salad with Strawberries, *58,* 59
  Chicken Salad Sandwiches, 88
White Rice, 126

Zucchini
  and Corn Salad, *62,* 63
  Parmesan Summer Squash, 146, *147*